M000016853

UNDERSTANDING THE SACRAMENTS

Rev. Peter M. J. Stravinskas

UNDERSTANDING THE SACRAMENTS

A Guide for Prayer and Study

IGNATIUS PRESS   SAN FRANCISCO

Excerpts from Scripture taken from the New American Bible
© 1970 by the Confraternity of Christian Doctrine,
Washington, D.C.

Based on *Understanding the Sacraments*,
© 1984 Twin Circle Publishing Company
All rights reserved

Reprinted with permission

Cover illustration by Renato Ortega

*The bird and grape motif dates from ancient classic times
and was adopted by the Early Church. The faithful are
symbolized by the birds who come to eat the grapes.
The grapes represent the Blood of Christ in the Eucharist.*

Cover design by Riz Boncan Marsella

Published by Ignatius Press, San Francisco, 1997
ISBN 0-89870-605-x
Library of Congress catalogue number 97-70805
Printed in the United States of America ∞

Contents

Foreword

The revelation of God in the New Testament is profoundly spiritual and interior. In light of this affirmation it might seem surprising that in the New Testament and in the life of the Church so much importance is given to material signs, surely sacred, but always belonging also to the material world. The apparent contradiction is easily overcome when, on the natural level, we acknowledge the importance of symbols in helping the multidimensional human person to perceive realities or values and, above all, when, on the faith level, we give full weight to the Incarnation of the Word.

The understanding of the sacraments that Fr. Stravinskas vigorously promotes in this book is intimately linked with the understanding of Christ. The author fortunately refers the reader again and again to the teachings of the *Catechism of the Catholic Church*. From these teachings, as well as from the documents of the Second Vatican Council, he draws the focus of the treatment: The sacraments are actions of Christ. It is

Christ who is active in the administration and reception of each sacrament. Each sacrament is an extension of his Paschal Mystery offered to the believer here and now. This Truth is indicated by the blood and water flowing from the Savior's wounded side, the fountain of sacramental life in the Church and, in particular, of Baptism and the Eucharist.

This so intimate relationship between Christ and the sacraments had been somewhat obscured by the order in which the theological treatises had been taught. The doctrine of the sacraments had been separated from christology by putting the whole of moral theology between the two. St. Thomas Aquinas, and now the *Catechism of the Catholic Church*, proposed a different order, in which the exposition of the Profession of Faith is immediately followed by Part Two, dealing with the celebration of the Christian Mystery in the sacramental economy. Fr. Stravinskas clearly and profoundly explains this intimate relationship between faith in Christ and the celebration of his Paschal Mystery in the liturgy, particularly in the sacraments. With the same intensity, the reader learns about the relationship of the sacraments to the Church, who is the guardian of the sacraments just as she is the custodian of the Scriptures and of the faith.

The sacred signs of the Church rightly are also called "the sacraments of faith", as they "not only presuppose faith, but by words and the elements of the rite they also nourish, strengthen and express it" (*Constitution on the Sacred Liturgy*, no. 59). The author, making use of his well-known theological formation and, at the same time, of his extensive pastoral experience, again and again insists not only on a positive understanding of the sacraments but also on the necessity of faithful observance of ecclesial rules. Thus he strongly encourages all to observe the diversity of rules and ministries in the administration of the sacraments, avoiding abuses that here and there have crept in—for instance, a wrong understanding and practice of extraordinary ministers of Holy Communion.

The whole book is of obvious timeliness. After each theme the author suggests questions for group discussion. These may serve as a tool to affirm the right understanding of the doctrine proposed and—why not here and there also—provide an opportunity for an examination of conscience. It may be underlined that the treatment of the Sacrament of Penance or Reconciliation, addressing therein also the themes of general absolution and First Penance before reception of the Eucharist, offers very timely clarifications. In the concluding questions the readers are asked: "Why do you think fewer people go to confession in our day?" Would it have been opportune to recall in this context the decisive role of the priests and their responsibility, if we deplore a diminished practice of so life-giving a sacrament? Do our priests preach enough of the healing, sanctifying, and strengthening grace, and do they render themselves lovingly and generously available to its administration?

Speaking of the Sacrament of Holy Orders, Fr. Stravinskas underlines that the priest, as an icon of Jesus Christ, is called to sacrifice his own life for the sake of the people. The priesthood exists for the Eucharist. In this light the relationship between the "royal priesthood" of all the faithful and the ministerial priesthood of some chosen by Christ, the tradition of priestly celibacy, and the specific functions of bishops and priests are addressed. In a substantial concluding point, Fr. Stravinskas enumerates thirteen elements of personal or communal life that keep us from appreciating in all their fullness the divine gifts of the sacraments of Christ. These pages appear most valuable for an appropriate examination of conscience, indicating at the same time avenues whereby we can contribute to a true renewal of Christian life as challenged by Vatican Council II and so vividly called for by our Holy Father in preparation for the great Jubilee Year 2000.

Thus not only by its title but also by its concise but rich content this "guide for prayer and study" can surely help to fulfill the wish of Vatican Council II, which declared it "of the highest importance that the faithful easily understand the sacramental signs, frequenting with great eagerness those sacraments which

were initiated to nourish the Christian life" (*Constitu-*
tion on the Sacred Liturgy, no. 59).

Paul Augustin Cardinal Mayer, O.S.B.

Rome, June 15, 1997

The Sacraments

Jesus Christ Is the First and Greatest Sacrament

G OD LOOKED at everything he had made, and he found it very good" (Gen 1:31; CCC 339). This realization provides the basis for the Church's insistence on a sacramental view of life.

From her earliest beginnings and at fairly regular intervals since, the Church has had to do battle against those who despise the material universe or those who wish to reduce the Church's mission to the level of the verbal or spiritual. Catholicism, however, true to its Jewish roots, looks upon man as a unified whole, in whom the material and the spiritual are so ordered that the individual is led to God (CCC 362–68).

The author of Psalm 19 knew this well in singing: "The heavens declare the glory of God, and the firmament proclaims his handiwork." Creation, then, is a sign of divine love and providence, something to be appreciated and used (Gen 1:24).

Throughout history, in every culture and religious experience, we find man making symbols and ritualizing the crucial aspects of his life (CCC 1146). It is in this sense that one can say that liturgy is natural to man. Since Christianity is an incarnational religion, it takes the multidimensional person seriously and thus offers a sacramental system whereby the physical leads the believer to know in the deepest sense the One who is spiritual (CCC 1076).

For the Christian, Jesus is the first and greatest sacrament (CCC 774) or sign man has ever received. He is the definitive sign of God's love for us and his last Word (Heb 1:1; CCC 65). In Christ are united both Word and sacrament, and it is thus that the Church accepts this paradigm for her own life. The Church herself is a sacrament of God's nearness to men and of his desire to save them (CCC 774–76). The sacramentality of the Church, rediscovered at Vatican II and proclaimed in *Lumen gentium*, provides the necessary linkage for the Church's seven sacraments: Jesus served as a sign of the Father; the Church is to be a sacrament of Christ in the world today; the seven sacraments give concrete expression to the Church's continuation of Christ's saving work among men (CCC 1099).

When we seek a definition of a sacrament, no better definition can be found than the one we learned in the Baltimore Catechism that "a sacrament is an outward sign, instituted by Christ to give grace" (CCC 1084, 1127, 1131).

The definition does need analysis, however.

When we speak of a sacrament as "an outward sign", we refer to the sensate nature of the human person, already described and alluded to in the opening lines of 1 John. In the natural order, certain phenomena carry automatic messages, though sometimes ambivalent messages. Rain can be welcome or unwelcome, depending on whether we are in the midst of a drought or a flood. A fire can signify warmth or destruction. In the supernatural order water, bread, wine, or oil always carries a clear and consistent message of salvation.

A Sign and a Symbol of a Deeper Reality

These signs, taken from the realm of human experience, transcend themselves when introduced into the Church's sacramental system (CCC 1145–55). Like the union of the human and divine natures in Christ, nature and "supernature" combine to produce a sign and a symbol of a deeper reality. Trained in the school of the Church and seeing with the eyes of faith, the sons and daughters of the Church are able to go beyond the ordinary in human experience to gain a glimpse of the divine.

An intelligent and truly Catholic understanding of the sacraments as "instituted by Christ" needs to avoid two extremes.

The first is a rather naïve and biblically indefensible position that holds that our Lord during his earthly life established each of the seven sacraments with their precise matter and form.

The second is a rationalistic approach that proposes that the Church's sacramental system is a mere ecclesiastical invention only remotely connected to the will of the Church's founder. A nuanced appreciation of the sacraments requires the realization that Christ the Lord established his Church, gave his life for her, and willed that the life-giving benefits of his Passion, death, and Resurrection be extended to all people of all time (CCC 1114–16).

Jesus wishes to touch our lives at all their critical points in concrete sacramental ways—just as he did during his earthly ministry. The Church, faithful to the Lord's commands, continues her saving work through sacramental signs (CCC 774). These rites have been adapted over the centuries, so that their salvific message may be better comprehended by the peoples of varying cultures and times. This kind of development steers the middle course between the two extremes, accounting for legitimate variations and yet opting for a sense of tradition that is faithful to the will of Christ (CCC 1204–9).

The Sacraments "Give Grace"

But what is grace? In the past, many thought of grace as a quantifiable object, so that one spoke of gaining "more grace". Without stooping to caricature, it would not be unfair to say that some Catholics have regarded the Church and the sacraments as some kind of spiritual "filling station". A far better view of grace is one that sees it as a relationship between the individual believer and Christ (CCC 2003). Thus, an increase in grace means a growth in one's relationship with the Lord. This type of explanation of sacramental life, interestingly enough, finds a very sympathetic hearing among many evangelical Protestants, who are so intent on the personal dimension of Christian life and faith.

How is grace obtained? Through a process of divine–human encounter and divine–human cooperation (CCC 2002). An analogy with the Incarnation might be helpful. When God sought a home among the human family, he approached the Blessed Virgin (the encounter) with his plan. As Mother Teresa says, she "gave God permission" (cooperation).

Catholic theology has always explained the operation of grace in the sacraments in exactly the same way. In every sacramental encounter, God takes the initiative by making the offer of grace (*ex opere operato*; cf. CCC 1128); the believer accepts the offer and opens himself up to the intervention of the divine (*ex opere operantis*). To hold both aspects in a healthy tension is necessary to avoid both a "magical" view of sacraments and one that places the human response above the divine call.

The Focus of Our Attention in the Sacraments

Vatican II's *Constitution on the Sacred Liturgy* emphasized a point frequently neglected or forgotten in regard to the celebration of the sacraments, namely, that it is Christ who is active in the administration and reception of each sacrament.

Each sacrament is an action of Christ and an extension of his Paschal Mystery offered to the believer in the here and now. It is not the priest, not the individual, and not even the Church that is the focus of our attention but Jesus himself. Priest, individual, and Church draw their meaning from Christ and are instruments and/or beneficiaries of his redemptive sacrifice—an important reminder in this day of personality cults (CCC 1127–28).

If all reality is sacramental, as I have suggested, then why bother with the sacraments? Because we need clear, unequivocal signs that cause what they signify.

The waters of Baptism, the oil of Confirmation, the bread of the Eucharist have a power to save, a power given to them by Christ himself and a power not given to nature in general or even to those same created things apart from the action of the Church. Salvation is sacramental (CCC 1076), this point subtly but beautifully stressed in the Gospel of John as we read of the blood and water flowing from the Savior's wounded side (Jn 20:34). The Church reminds us on the Solemnity of the Sacred Heart that this was "the fountain of sacramental life in the Church" (Preface), symbolizing the gifts of Baptism and Eucharist.

To have a valid celebration of a sacrament, one must have: a validly ordained minister who intends to do what the Church intends, a believer, and the correct matter and form of the rite (CCC 1128). These prerequisites are not designed to make difficult a sacramental encounter but rather to ensure its occurrence. The Church is the custodian of the sacraments (CCC 1118), just as she is the custodian of the Scriptures. She guards them carefully for the sake of her members, so that access to Christ will be possible in every age and at every moment.

Word and Sacrament Complement Each Other

Catholics have traditionally had a very highly developed sacramental sense, while Protestants have tended to stress the importance of the Bible. These emphases are not antagonistic to each other or mutually exclusive. In fact, they are complementary. From historical documents we know that Luther defined the Church as that place where the Word of God is preached and the sacraments duly administered. We also know that for all its emphasis on the sacraments, the Council of Trent likewise called for a renewal of Catholic preaching. Vatican II, without apology, asserted that Catholics have always reverenced the Sacred Scriptures as they have the Lord's Body (CCC 103). Just as the Word became flesh in the Incarnation, so too a celebration of God's Word necessarily leads to its "enfleshment" in a sacramental rite (CCC 1153–55).

Other Christians are beginning to accept this sacramentality of ours as the uniquely Catholic contribution to the ecumenical movement. There is cause for rejoicing here because the sacraments can now be a source of unity rather than division.

The sacraments are signs of the inbreaking of God's kingdom (cf. CCC 1107). Eastern Christian theology has always regarded the liturgy as an experience of heaven on earth; Vatican II referred to it as "a foretaste of the heavenly liturgy". The sacraments are the helps offered to God's people as they make their journey home to the Father, as individuals and as a community.

These sacramental encounters with Christ now point toward that eternal encounter in which there will be no need of sacraments because God will be "all in all" (Col 3:11). Until that day, though, we celebrate the sacraments, thanking God for those rites that proclaim so clearly, so dramatically, and so beautifully that our God is involved and that he cares.

Questions for Group Discussion

1. What exactly is a sacrament?
2. Why is it appropriate to describe Jesus and the Church as sacraments?
3. What are the two positions we should avoid in seeking to understand the sacraments?
4. How do the sacraments dispense God's grace to us?
5. What is necessary to have a valid celebration of a sacrament? Why?

Baptism

Understanding the Significance of Our Rebirth in All Its Beauty

EASTERTIDE is the season in which we traditionally focus our attention on Baptism, the sacrament of rebirth and new life. Whether one was baptized as an infant or as an adult, the meaning of this first sacrament of initiation needs to be explored again and again to attain a true appreciation of its power. If I were to ask the average parents presenting their child for Baptism why they do so, I can safely say that 95 percent would suggest the removal of original sin as their reason. And they would be right—however, they would not be going far enough. Our goal should be to understand the significance of Baptism in all its beauty.

Everyone who comes into this world possesses a weakened human nature, not a corrupt nature, but one that is inclined to do its own will rather than God's (CCC 407–9). The original sin of our first parents is washed away in the saving waters of Baptism (CCC 1250). That first, necessary step having been taken, the sacrament then disposes the person to hear and accept God's Word (CCC 1266). It incorporates him into the Church, that community of faith which will provide the environment for living out his baptismal promises (CCC 1267–70).

It is good to recall that the first Christians were adult converts who were able to declare their own intentions. Today, infants are the usual recipients of Baptism, a phenomenon attacked in some quarters as bad theology or even bad psychology. Such questions lead us to ask ourselves the precise meaning of infant Baptism.

The Meaning of Infant Baptism

This ancient practice of the Church says many things (CCC 1250–52). First and foremost, it reminds us that the gift of faith is just that—a gift on which we can never make a claim. God's love is so great that he offers himself to us before we can ever return his love. Secondly, we learn that the Lord withholds his love from no one. Intelligence is not a prerequisite; only an attitude of openness is. And who is more open or deserving than a child? Surely this was one reason Christ urged the apostles to allow the little ones to come to him (Mk 10:14–16). Interestingly, some exegetes see in this passage Mark's answer to those who questioned the practice of baptizing children when whole households were received into the Church (for example, Acts 16:15). Finally, we know that good parents always wish to provide their children with the best of everything, so that they may experience a full and happy life. If anything is crucial to a life of meaning and value, it is that God be included in that life. Therefore, having already shared the gift of life with their children, parents are then called upon to share the gift of faith.

Infant Baptism is a powerful statement of our belief in divine initiative and divine election. Just as the Jews are born into the Chosen People simply by virtue of their parentage and not due to their own worthiness, we Christians are born into a family of faith because of God's grace and providence, and never by our own doing—even if one is an adult convert.

Another related question is sometimes raised by parents whose child has died without Baptism: "What will happen to my baby?" The simplest answer might be that the desire of the parents that this infant become a child of God is a type of Baptism in itself. Furthermore, it is important to note that we (or even the Church) cannot limit God's love, mercy, and compassion to human (and even ecclesiastical) formulations, for God's ways are not our ways (Is 55:8). St. Thomas Aquinas felt compelled to remind his readers that "Deus non alligatur sacramentis [God is not bound to the sacraments]." That is, although the sacraments are surely the ordinary means of grace, they are not the only means by which God can effect our salvation. And so, we commend such a child to God's fatherly care (CCC 1261).

The theological principle "legem credendi statuit lex orandi [the rule of prayer determines the rule of faith]" informs us that there is a correlation between Christian prayer and Christian belief (CCC 1124). The liturgy of Baptism provides a full explanation of what the Church understands to be happening in this sacred rite. For this reason, it would be most worthwhile to examine it in some detail.

The Sacred Rite of Baptism

The most obvious symbol is the water (CCC 1238). However, most people have an impoverished understanding of its meaning. It signifies cleansing from original sin, yes; but it also means much more. Water is an element that can bring death or life. During the Exodus experience the same waters that brought salvation to the Hebrews brought death to the Egyptians. In the early Church, the person to be baptized was plunged into the water to symbolize death to sin and selfishness; when he arose from the water, he emerged a new man in the likeness of Christ. Our Baptism is both the Exodus experience and the Paschal Mystery.

So much of the idea of a new beginning is echoed again and again in the baptismal liturgy. The child is presented with a white garment, which reminds us of a new-found innocence and also of that "new man" with whom St. Paul urged us to clothe ourselves (Eph 4:24; CCC 1243). The priest may touch the ears and lips of the newly baptized in imitation of our Lord, who made the deaf to hear and the dumb to speak. Henceforth, this child will be ready to hear and accept the Word of God and to proclaim it with the aid of the whole Church, the communion of saints. And so, we seek the assistance of all the saints and pray that this child's patron may serve as an example to inspire this new Christian to live totally for God.

The child is anointed with oil, the same sacred chrism with which priests, prophets, and kings were anointed in the Old Testament. This dedicates the child to God and gives him a role in the priestly people formed by Jesus Christ, which is his Church (CCC 1241). Having put on the "new man" and having received the commission to hear and spread the gospel, the child, through his parents, is given the candle lighted from the Easter candle (which symbolizes the light of Christ; CCC 1243), for it is in his light that this child must walk if he is to attain the salvation promised.

The parents are at the very heart of things in the new rite (CCC 1251). One of the most positive de-

velopments in baptismal practice in the renewal process has been the emphasis on the parents and the assistance given to them in baptismal preparation
programs. In the "old days" parents were often looked
upon as "in the way" at a Baptism (if they were allowed to be present at all). The new rite remedies that
deficiency and places the parents at the very heart of
things—where they belong. Much of the burden is
on the parents at this point. They renounce sin and
profess faith; it is their responsibility to see to it that
their lives give testimony to the faith they have pro-
fessed, for they will be the first Christian influence on
this child.

But parents also need help. The godparents can be
looked upon as a kind of link to the extended family
of the Church, which pledges support in bringing the
newly baptized to a vigorous life of faith (CCC 1255).
Later on, the parents can also seek the Church's help by
entrusting their children to a Catholic school, so that
the values they have begun to share will be positively
and consistently reinforced in the educational environment (CCC 2229).

Although all Christians acknowledge the critical
importance of Baptism, not all interpret its effects in
the same way. Some Christians would see this ritual as
the culmination of the conversion experience; we
Catholics see it as only the beginning (CCC 1253–54).
For us, growth in faith and in our relationship with

Christ and his Church is essential, requiring an on-
going daily process of recommitment.

Each time we enter a church building, we bless ourselves with the water that recalls our Baptism, by
which we entered the Church, which is the Body of
Christ (CCC 1267, 1668). This sign is an indication of
our continued willingness to be faithful to our baptismal promises to die to sin and to live only for God; it
is a prayer that the Lord, who began this good work of
salvation within us on the day of our Baptism, will also
bring it to completion in the life of heaven.

Questions for Group Discussion

1. What is the purpose of Baptism?
2. Why does the Church insist on the practice of infant Baptism?
3. How is the theme of new life highlighted through
   the symbols used in administering Baptism?

3

Confirmation

*Turning Outward with a Concern for
the Salvation of the World*

THE SACRAMENT of the Holy Spirit, the sacrament
of completion, the sacrament of maturity, the
sacrament of Christian witness. All of these descrip-
tions are attempts to capture the essence of Confirmation, but, like the Spirit himself, this sacrament cannot
be pinned down and neatly compartmentalized. And
so, we conclude that Confirmation is all these things—
and more.

Confirmation is the sealing of the baptismal commitment, or better, the baptismal covenant (CCC
1285; 1295–96). Because of this close link, much of
the same symbolism is repeated. To highlight this connection, the revised Code of Canon Law urges that the
Confirmation sponsor ideally be the same person who
stood up for the candidate at Baptism (CCC 1131).

It has become common to explain this sacrament as

the personal affirmation of one's Baptism. While there is much to recommend this approach, we must also be careful not to overstress the role of the recipient. Therefore, it is necessary to view this sacrament as the action of the Spirit sent by Jesus to be our Paraclete, as well as the action of the whole Church begging her Lord to overtake this person completely with his gifts of grace. Confirmation gives the Christian permanent and full status in the family of the Church (CCC 1303, 1316).

The History behind Confirmation

In the early Church, the sacraments of Baptism, Confirmation, and Eucharist were all received together, forming a unified rite of Christian initiation (CCC 1212, 1290, 1298, 1306). This sequence is still followed by the Eastern rites of the Church, so that even babies are baptized, chrismated (confirmed), and communicated (although a child's "second Communion" is often delayed to the age of reason).

In the Latin rite, certain ethnic groups preserved this order of the sacraments, although they spread them out over a period of years. Some readers may recall that they were confirmed at the age of ten, and only at some later date did they receive their First Holy Communion.

The notion behind this practice is that it seemed

strange to allow the reception of the Eucharist before one was a "full-fledged" member of the Church. The new Code of Canon Law appears to envision a rather early age for Confirmation, unless the national bishops' conference decrees otherwise. However, the point about full membership in the Church should not be pushed to an extreme, for Baptism does indeed incorporate the believer into the Body of Christ (the Church). Thus, reception of the Body of Christ (the Eucharist) is not really out of order.

As a successor of the apostles, the bishop (except in certain circumstances) administers Confirmation to highlight the relationship between the first Pentecost in the early Church and our own personal Pentecost experienced through this sacrament today. The bishop's presence also illustrates that the faith we make our own goes back to the teachings of the apostles. Therefore, Confirmation not only stresses the unity of the Church's members today but also points out our unity with all believers throughout the ages.

An interesting historical anomaly is that while the Eastern Churches have preserved the original order of the sacraments of initiation, it is a priest who is their ordinary minister (CCC 1290, 1312). Although the Latin rite has separated the three sacraments from each other and changed their order, it has maintained the bishop as the ordinary minister of Confirmation (CCC 1290, 1292, 1313). In an effort to keep some relationship among the three sacraments of initiation, the Latin rite calls for the renewal of baptismal promises during the Confirmation ceremony and sees the administration of the sacrament as ideally situated within the context of the Mass.

From earliest times a special ritual for the imparting of the Holy Spirit is in evidence (cf. Acts 8:14; 19:6). However, even theologians are sometimes hard-pressed to explain the differences between Baptism and Confirmation. Some suggest that the degree of incorporation into the Church is the difference, which has already been discussed. Others locate the uniqueness of Confirmation in its being the preeminent sacrament of the Holy Spirit, or in the communication to the recipient of the gifts and fruits of the Spirit. However, the Spirit is operative in all the sacraments (CCC 1091–92). So perhaps the best way to look at the situation is through the recipient and the sacrament's effect.

The Work of the Holy Spirit

The special work theology traditionally assigns to the third Person of the Blessed Trinity is that of sanctification. In Confirmation the recipient is given a particular grace to be open to the operation of the Spirit, so that there is a special turning to the Spirit in the same way that our Lord, Mary, and the apostles opened themselves up to the promptings of the Spirit and thus performed the works of the Spirit (CCC 1303). Baptism is concerned with the salvation of the individual; Confirmation takes that saved individual and turns him outward with concern for the salvation of the world.

Through the ancient biblical gesture of the imposition of hands, the ritual formula ("Be sealed with the Gift of the Holy Spirit"; CCC 1300, 1320), and the anointing with chrism, the Christian is marked with a special, permanent character, setting him apart for a life of public witness (CCC 1304, 1317). The Anglican theologian William Temple once observed that "the Church exists for those who are not yet members of her." This insight is particularly useful here. A Christian vocation that is not missionary is, by its very nature, defective. A living out of one's baptismal and Confirmation commitments requires one to share the gospel with others and to invite others to experience the fullness of life known only through membership in the Church.

Answers to Three Modern Questions

The Sacrament of Confirmation helps provide some answers for three modern questions, questions relating to the priesthood of the faithful, the approximate age for reception of the sacrament, and the need for continuing theological education.

In "the old days" we used to speak of Confirmation as making people into soldiers of Christ (cf. CCC 1295). One may balk at such military imagery, but an important point was being made—namely, that Confirmation gave a Catholic certain responsibilities, that one was sent on a mission.

This work includes both "offensive" and "defensive" elements, to continue with the military metaphor. Offensively, it means making a positive effort to communicate the gospel message and the significance of life in the Church, most especially through the joyful example of a good Christian life (CCC 1305). Included in this form of witness is reaching out to others and asking them to consider life in the Church. While this may be characterized as taking the offensive, it should never be done aggressively but rather with sensitivity, charity, and respect for the dignity of the other.

Defensively, it means providing an explanation of Church teachings, particularly when they are misunderstood or misrepresented. Questions from inquirers should not be perceived as attacks on oneself or on the Church but as a genuine effort to come to a knowledge of the truth.

This twofold process, of course, is that of attracting converts to the Church—one of the most important areas for lay involvement and the one most sadly and frequently neglected today. Priests would generally agree that the vast numbers of converts brought into

the Church in the 1950s came through committed
laypeople who took seriously the responsibilities
flowing from their Baptism and Confirmation. After
the apostles received the Gift of the Holy Spirit on
Pentecost Sunday, they immediately went out to
preach with courage and conviction. The result, St.
Luke tells us, was that three thousand people were
added to the Church that day. Confirmation does indeed give its grace to the individual for the salvation
of the world.

The First Epistle of Peter speaks of Christians as a
royal priesthood and a people set apart from their pagan environment (CCC 901, 1141, 1268). They are to
be "countercultural agents", living in the world but
not being a part of it. Within the entire priestly people,
by divine plan, one finds a special ministerial priesthood whose specific task it is to nourish the entire
Church with Word and sacrament. If ordained priests
fulfill their ministry, the laity will serve as "priests" to
the world, in their turn. Confirmation strengthens
Christians to assume their rightful place in the midst
of that entire priestly people, which is the Church of
Jesus Christ.

When should one receive this "sacrament of maturity"? Infant Baptism is a beautiful and ancient tradition in the Church, but we must admit that it poses
one serious difficulty: At some future moment, a child
will have to affirm personally all the values and beliefs

he has received. In recent years, this awareness has led to a renewed emphasis on the Sacrament of Confirmation. Careful preparation of candidates is vital, to ensure that they understand what they are about to do and also that they really want to do this (CCC 1309). Confirmation can never simply be another social amenity or else it will devolve into a meaningless ritual. Maturity and conviction must be demanded of every candidate.

However, two cautions seem in order. First, most parents and educators agree that the attainment of maturity is a highly individualized phenomenon (CCC 1308). Therefore, hard-and-fast rules would appear to be imprudent and at times even unjust. Secondly, in recent years we have seen demands made on Confirmation candidates that are sometimes so excessive as to make preparation for the sacrament unpleasant and at times nearly impossible. As in so many areas of life, a sensible middle road must be used in how and when a young person is made ready for the sacrament.

One final consideration is the necessity for growth in one's understanding of the Catholic faith. So often people end their theological education the day they are confirmed or leave a Catholic school for the last time. Such people may have a doctorate in physics but only the most rudimentary grasp of their faith. This is embarrassing to the Church and should be embarrassing to the individual.

The Spirit received in Confirmation is, above all, the Spirit of Truth (Jn 14:26; 15:26; 16:13), whom Jesus promised as a teacher for his Church. The ongoing presence of a teacher implies the ongoing presence of students, and all members of Christ's Church need constant education in the things of faith. This process can occur through formal classes, through the private and prayerful study of the Scriptures, or through a deliberate, personal program of reading the history of the Church, the lives of the saints, the teachings of the Magisterium today, and the writings of good Catholic authors.

Although this is a serious obligation resulting from one's Confirmation, it should also be seen as a privilege and joy. *Fides quaerens intellectum* (faith seeking understanding) has always been the Catholic way because a growth in knowledge leads the believer to a deeper appreciation of the object of faith—the Beloved himself (CCC 158). Continuous education in faith, then, is a lifelong commitment taken up with the assistance of the Spirit of Truth, who is received in a special way in Confirmation.

Several times in the Gospel of John, the Holy Spirit is referred to as the Paraclete, a Greek word with a double meaning: advocate (defense attorney) and judge (CCC 692). The evangelist did not choose this word haphazardly but with purpose, for the Holy Spirit is indeed both our advocate and judge. He pleads our cause but also judges us. The permanent character of Confirmation, which marks us off as a chosen people, works in much the same way. On the Last Day that sacramental seal will be a witness for us or against us, depending on how well we have responded to the special graces we have received.

The hope of the Church is that all her children live their lives in such fidelity to the grace of this sacrament that they deserve to have the Holy Spirit as a most kindly Advocate.

Questions for Group Discussion

1. If the Holy Spirit is active in all the sacraments, how does one explain his special activity in Confirmation?

2. Why is Confirmation considered a sacrament of initiation?

3. What do the permanent character of Confirmation and the grace of the sacrament do for a Christian? What are the responsibilities of a confirmed Catholic?

4. Identify the gifts and fruits of the Holy Spirit that are given in a special way at Confirmation. See especially Isaiah 11:2 and Galatians 5:22. Discuss their operation in your life. What is the primary difference between the Isaian gifts of the Holy Spirit and the Pauline fruits of the Holy Spirit in Galatians?

5. What is the double meaning of the Greek word *paraclete*? How does it illuminate the role of the Holy Spirit in the lives of those who have been confirmed?

4

The Eucharist

Through the Consecrated Bread and Wine,
Jesus Remains with Us Now and Forever

How does the believer maintain contact with the Risen Christ? Did the first apostles and disciples of Jesus have an advantage over those to follow in developing a relationship of intimacy with the Lord?

Such questions have been matters of concern to Christians throughout the ages, and even within the New Testament itself we get hints of such concern. We also see how the sacred writers attempted to answer those questions.

The sixth chapter of John's Gospel deals with such issues insightfully and effectively. But Luke does so with poetry, art, and sensitivity. He tells a story. The Emmaus passage (Lk 24:13–35) is a story of rare charm and beauty and teaches theology by means of a drama. To the plea of the disciples ("stay with us"), the Stranger responds, not with a dissertation, but with a ritual, familiar action ("the breaking of the bread"). At the very moment the disciples recognize their Guest as the Risen One, he vanishes from their sight.

What is Luke's point? This story is his answer to the two questions we noted at the outset. The contemporary disciple encounters the Risen Christ in the Eucharist. And, no, those disciples of yesteryear who walked and talked with Jesus during his earthly life had no advantage over us today, because we encounter the very same Christ that they did. The proof is that Jesus in his glorious and risen body disappears the minute the disciples recognize him in the signs and symbols of the Eucharist, for the physical Christ is a redundancy when the sacramental Christ is present.

In *The Elusive Presence,* Samuel Terrien demonstrates that the whole of the divine–human relationship chronicled in the Scriptures is one of progressive intimacy: from the conversations between God and Adam in Eden, to the covenant with Abraham, to the giving of the Law, to the Incarnation. In fact, the story of God's involvement with his people is merely the fulfillment of his desire to be near to those he loves. The Eucharist is the special way that the Lord Jesus makes good on his promise to be with us until the end of time (cf. Mt 28:30).

Just what is the Eucharist? Definitions are always inadequate, but let us hazard this one: The Eucharist is a sacrificial meal commemorating and offering salvation.

It is the "making present" again of the Lord's Supper in which Jesus realizes his destiny, committing himself to his act of self-giving in fidelity and love (CCC 1323).

The Significance of the Eucharist as a Meal

Jesus chose a meal to do this for many reasons. A meal is a very significant human experience. One shares a table only with friends and family; inviting someone to dinner is an expression of esteem. Jews looked on a meal as a ritual action, and the particular meal that Jesus chose (the Passover) was replete with religious meaning. By using the Passover meal, Jesus could take advantage of past Jewish history to illustrate what he was about to do; because of its religious and instructional character, he could teach his disciples the basics of being his follower (cf. Jn 13–17; Lk 22:14–36; CCC 1339–40). Familiarity with the twelfth chapter of Exodus is most beneficial for a proper understanding of the Christian Eucharist, for notions like blood, sacrifice, lamb, and memorial feast have their roots firmly planted in the Passover experience.

The Perfect and Acceptable Sacrifice

Thus the Last Supper points toward Calvary, where all men of all time were saved (cf. Heb 9). If all people were saved in that one momentous occasion, why does the Church continue to offer the Sacrifice of the Mass? Because the salvation promised and earned is conditional; it is contingent upon our acceptance of Jesus, our desire to be saved, and a lifestyle that demonstrates our understanding of what life in Christ means. Because we were not present, we need to be reminded of what God has done for us. Our remembrance and ritual reenactment of the event make it happen again —for us (CCC 1362–67).

Jesus offers his Body and Blood; his death brings us life, just as the blood of the lamb saved the Hebrews. Washed in his Blood, we are cleansed from sin (cf. Heb 9:14) and made alive to God's design for our salvation. Receiving the Body of Christ makes each of us as individuals to form the Body of Christ, which is his Church (CCC 1396). In other words, the eucharistic Body of Christ is offered to us, so that we can become more clearly the Body of Christ as the Church. Herein lies the Catholic rationale for refusing to practice intercommunion, that is, receiving Communion with other Christians (CCC 1398–1401). This sacrament celebrates union with Christ but also union with the Church. To feign such unity, when significant differences of doctrine and belief separate us as Catholics from full communion with other Christians, is to make of the Eucharist a countersign.

How does the marvelous exchange of gifts occur—

Christ for bread and wine? Jesus told us to remember him, for memory is a most powerful human faculty. For a Jew, to remember someone or some event was to represent the benefits of that relationship. That is why, of all Christ's commandments, the one to remember him is the most critical. If we fail to remember Jesus, if we fail to renew his sacrificial meal, we will cease to be Christians because we will no longer hear those words of love, no longer receive his Body and Blood as their proof, no longer be challenged and inspired to love our fellowman as he commanded us. Therefore, memory is key; sacred memory leads us to sacred reality.

The Words of Consecration

Furthermore, when the Church gathers in faith to do what Jesus commanded and speak his words, "this is my Body to be given up for you. . . . This cup is the new covenant of my Blood which will be shed for you . . .", our words are no longer our own but God's. The Word overtakes the elements of bread and wine and transforms them into the divine Presence (CCC 1373–77, 1413). Jesus our God comes among us again. Through faith, we acknowledge him as present and look forward to that time when he will come again in glory and no longer under veiled signs.

The Jesus who comes to us in this mysterious manner also remains with us under the sacred signs. For this reason, the Church has always encouraged devotion to the Blessed Sacrament (CCC 1378, 1418). We come to the Christ of the Eucharist with our present sorrows, and we ask him to unite them to his, which were nailed to the Cross. For through the Cross, we hope to share in the Resurrection. The eucharistic Jesus is a consolation but also a challenge: to be all that we are meant to be, to become one family because we are fed with one Bread, to love one another as he has loved us.

The Controversies surrounding the Eucharist

Ironically enough, this sacrament of unity and peace has so often been a sacrament of division, in the sense that so many controversies have surrounded its interpretation. Our age is no different.

Some Christians, for example, argue that the Eucharist is merely a symbolic feeding. But even a cursory reading of John 6 reveals that our Lord meant the Eucharist to be understood and received as his very Body and Blood. How else explain the negative reaction of the crowd and their subsequent departure from his company (cf. Jn 6:59 and 67; CCC 1336)? How else explain martyrs giving their lives rather than profane the sacred species? No, we are in touch with something very real here.

Others question the sacrificial nature of the Eucharist, holding for only a sacred meal. The meal aspect is, of course, important. However, the meal takes its significance from the sacrifice. This is most obvious from all the scriptural texts that speak of the Body to be given up and the Blood to be poured out as future events. Holy Thursday's covenantal meal of promise is fulfilled in Good Friday's covenantal sacrifice (cf. 1 Cor 11:26).

Is it possible to receive the Eucharist too often? Perhaps the better way to frame the question is: Are there times when one should not receive the Eucharist? The answer is a clear and resounding "yes": when one is in the state of mortal sin or when one is engaged in a mere routine action (CCC 1385). It has always been a source of distress to priests that so many people now approach the altar with little or no preparation or examination of conscience. The Holy Father alluded to this recently in noting that the phenomenon of increased reception of the Eucharist is positive only if these frequent encounters are worthy. In this he merely echoed St. Paul's concerns of two millennia ago (1 Cor 11:38).

Like the disciples on the road to Emmaus, we invite the Unknown Guest to stay with us. And, like them, we are led to recognize that neither Peter nor Mary Magdalen was any better off than we, for, like the Blessed Virgin herself, we bear Christ within our very selves—through the gift of the Eucharist.

The Proper Use of Extraordinary Ministers

When may a nonordained person distribute Holy Communion? According to *Immensae caritatis* (Pope Paul VI's decree permitting this practice) and the revised Code of Canon Law, only under the following clearly defined circumstances: the lack of an ordinary minister of the Eucharist (bishop, priest, or deacon); the inability of an ordinary minister to function because of ill health or advanced age; an unwieldy number of communicants with an insufficient number of ordinary ministers.

The Abuse of the Church's Teaching on Extraordinary Ministers of the Eucharist

In an article on lay ministry some time ago, one American Catholic newsweekly observed that on any given Sunday in the United States more Catholics receive Communion from the hands of a layperson than from a priest or deacon. While this is probably an exaggeration, experience proves it close to true.

Over a three-year period, I preached in more than one hundred parishes at weekend Masses; only seven did not use extraordinary ministers of the Eucharist—and none, to the best of my knowledge, fulfilled the requirements of *Immensae caritatis*. Some places have literally dozens of people so deputed (I know of one parish that has 225 extraordinary ministers of the Eucharist). And it is not unusual for people in the pews to observe that some of these ministers lead less than exemplary Christian lives; some of them are even divorced and remarried.

The unwillingness to use the word "extraordinary" ("special" is a frequent designation) in reference to these ministers is common and suggests an imprudent desire to make this ministry both ordinary and accepted. Furthermore, other titles have crept in—lay eucharistic ministers and, even more theologically unsound, bread ministers and wine ministers. A brief survey of schedules in parish bulletins would show the extent of their use and the confusion of titles.

It is interesting to note here that no other church or ecclesial community professing belief in the Real Presence, such as Lutherans and Episcopalians, permits laypeople to distribute the Sacred Host.

It also seems clear that *Immensae caritatis* had behind it good intentions, but the lived reality in the United States has had negative consequences. This is one of the most serious problems to emerge in the postconciliar Church in America, since it touches on the very heart of Catholic faith and practice ("the source and summit of the Christian life", as Vatican II refers to the liturgy) in a most visible way, affecting every Catholic.

First, several items in brief—some sad, others merely strange. In some parishes, the sick now receive the ministrations of a priest (especially the Sacrament of Penance) only irregularly, if at all, forcing them to feel abandoned and marginalized from the mainstream of Church life.

Another example: Although the number of communicants probably peaked around 1968, no complaints were heard about "long" Communion lines. Yet some liturgists argue the necessity of having laypeople as ministers of Holy Communion by suggesting that the distribution of Communion should not exceed seven minutes. The height of irony is reached, however, when some celebrants sit for a meditation period of roughly that length after Communion.

In some parishes it has become routine to have laypeople assist with Communion, regardless of the number of communicants or available clergy, even for small daily Mass congregations. Due to the extensive use of extraordinary ministers and laypeople performing other functions, many parishioners see their priests only when they are celebrants of the Mass at the altar. This means that priests are absent from their people at the peak moments of parish life. On the other hand, in not a few parishes priests are available to greet the people before and after Sunday liturgy—but are not available for distributing Communion.

A Lost Sense of the Sacred and a Distorted View of the Lay Apostolate

The improper use of extraordinary ministers of the Eucharist is, of course, a violation of correct liturgical procedure and sometimes a deliberate act of defiance. However, two other serious problems also present themselves: a lost sense of the sacred and a distorted view of the lay apostolate.

Throughout this book, we have been attempting to highlight the sacramental, incarnational aspects of Catholic life in their uniqueness. Underpinning all of this is that we must have a deep sense of the sacred. The making of distinctions contributes to that sense: What we wear to the beach is inappropriate for church; the rock music of the radio is out of place in a worship service. Were we not to distinguish in this way, all of life would be a plateau, with no mountains and no valleys.

By permitting nearly anyone at all to distribute the Eucharist, we are communicating a message at the symbolic level that this action is really not all that special. What is anyone's responsibility is no one's responsibility. Surely that is what young boys mean when they say they are not interested in the priesthood because "anybody can do what you guys do."

The usual reason given for the use of extraordinary ministers of the Eucharist (namely, time constraints) fosters the American "in and out" mentality of Sunday Mass. The effect is to blur distinctions of any kind in the Church, forgetting that such distinctions are natural to man. This approach, though almost always innocent, nonetheless culminates in a desacralization of the Church, the Eucharist, and the priesthood. We have already seen strong indications of this development, and that is why Pope John Paul II (in *Dominicae cenae*) criticized the abuse of the permission for extraordinary ministers as "reprehensible". Interestingly enough, the desacralization of religion does not increase our appreciation of life in general, rather, it vulgarizes both.

One final area of concern revolves around the significance of the lay apostolate. It never ceases to amaze me as a priest that when I invite people to become active in the work of the Church, almost invariably they volunteer for liturgical ministries. This demonstrates that Vatican II is still not fully understood. The whole point of the Council's theology of the laity was that the laity have their own unique role to play in bringing the gospel to contemporary humanity—in the world, not in the sanctuary.

The Church operates, at the sociological level, on the principle of a "division of labor" (CCC 1348). Theologically, this is referred to as a "diversity of roles and ministries". St. Paul expressed this in his analogy of the Church with the human body (1 Cor 12:12–22).

Of course, all members are equal, but not all have the same function. Equality is not sameness. To reduce the living out of one's baptismal commitment to a sacramental ministry is to mistake the part for the whole. It also involves serious role confusion. The role of the priest is to preach and administer the sacraments, so that the laity can be faithful witnesses in the world, thus inviting people there to follow Christ (CCC 1142-44).

In terms of lay participation in the liturgy, a diversity of roles also exists. To suggest that full liturgical participation requires lay ministers of the Eucharist is to misunderstand this point. To be present and to take an active part in the singing and praying is full participation; anything else is a strange form of anticlericalism, which is really very clericalistic at root: the desire of the laity to be priests themselves! In his Bicentennial Message to the United States, Paul VI reminded us that the role of extraordinary ministers is not "the ordinary expression of lay participation".

This confusion is so deep-seated now, however, that one bishop in a pastoral letter on the liturgy argued that the use of extraordinary ministers of the Eucharist proclaims the basic unity of all around the table of the Lord. I must disagree with that point, which is clericalism at its worst. Baptism makes us one (CCC 1267)—not the act of gaining access to a ciborium. In some dioceses pastors have been forced to use these ministers as a sign of their acceptance of "Vatican II" or "the priesthood of the faithful". Yet, ironically, all the arguments brought forth to justify this practice actually diminish the noble calling of Christian laypersons and suggest that the only real Catholics are priests or at least people who do "priestly" things.

Please note that we are not concerned with heresy here but with an imprudent, unwise liturgical practice, reflective of bad sociology. Like other Americanisms in the Church, this one fails to take a holistic view of reality, neglects long-range implications, and does not take seriously the nonverbal, symbolic power of liturgical communication.

The only solution to this grave pastoral problem is for bishops and laity alike to insist that *Immensae caritatis* be carefully followed. The decree itself reminds clergy of their important obligations here:

> Since these faculties are granted only for the spiritual good of the faithful and for cases of genuine necessity, priests are to remember that they are not thereby excused from the task of distributing the Eucharist to the faithful who legitimately request it.

The correct interpretation of this decree will result in an increased reverence for the Eucharist as well as an increased reverence for the apostolate of the laity.

Questions for Group Discussion

1. What exactly is the Eucharist? Describe its main elements in your own words.

2. Why does the Catholic Church refuse to practice intercommunion?

3. Explain the connection between Word and Sacrament in the Eucharist.

4. When should extraordinary ministers be used to distribute Holy Communion?

5. What should our attitude of heart and mind be when we receive the Eucharist?

Penance

Peace Begins with Our Personal Desire to Repent

THE FIRST WORD uttered by the Risen Christ was his Easter gift to his Church: "Peace!"

It is significant that immediately following that greeting is the Lord's commission to his apostles to forgive sins in his name: "If you forgive men's sins, they are forgiven; if you hold them bound, they are held bound" (Jn 20:23). What is the connection between the two statements?

Shalom, the Hebrew word Jesus would have used that first Easter night, carries within itself so many meanings that it cannot be adequately translated by a single word. *Shalom* connotes wholeness, harmony, unity, peace, and right relationships. It harks back to the Genesis accounts that depict God and man in an intimate union of friendship (CCC 374).

That union was destroyed, however, by the sin of our first parents (CCC 399). From that day on, sin has always obstructed the movement of man toward God (CCC 409). For peace to be found, the roadblock of sin must be removed. Hence the link between the Resurrection gift of peace and the Resurrection gift of forgiveness.

That link is maintained by the Church in the Sacrament of Penance (CCC 1468). Not without reason did many of the Fathers of the Church refer to Penance as "the second Baptism". They saw in this sacrament the consoling possibility of returning to baptismal innocence, the ability to have a second chance if one is only willing to repent and begin again.

How We Should Prepare to Receive the Sacrament

Before approaching the Sacrament of Penance, it is important for the believer to prepare properly: examination of conscience; sorrow for sin; firm purpose of amendment (CCC 1450–54). These steps are essential if our reception of the sacrament is to be a true encounter between the sinful self and the forgiving Christ. Nothing less than a true desire to turn from sin, to change one's life, to go through a conversion experience is required.

Frequently, other Christians have the misconception that our approach to sin is one of: "Oh well, I'll just go to confession on Saturday." But such an attitude mocks God's justice and is a parody of Catholic sacramental theology.

After preparing, the penitent is ready to receive the sacrament by the confession of sins to a priest and the performance of an appropriate work of satisfaction (CCC 1455–60). It is in these two areas that the celebration of the sacrament has so often changed throughout history.

How the Practice of Penance Has Changed in the Church

For many years in the early Church, Penance could be received only once in a lifetime. As a result, most people postponed its reception until they thought death was near. Eventually the Church increased the number of times Penance could be received to the point of our present observance, under which it is almost available "on demand".

Another interesting historical note is that in the early Church, all penance given for sins was "public penance", which meant that the entire Christian community was aware of the sinfulness of one of its members. Sinners were admitted to the "order of penitents" by the local bishop to perform penances involving corporal mortification, often extended over months or even years; the mere recitation of a prayer was not sufficient.

In due time, the discipline of the sacrament was again relaxed as Church thinking about Penance developed. Public penance was abolished, and a penitent could confess his sins to any priest who had received the authority of his bishop to forgive sins in the name of the Church. This practice became known as "private" or "auricular" confession (CCC 1447).

The privacy gained under this system was most welcome, but an important insight became obscured: Every sin (no matter how personal) diminishes the other members of the Body of Christ, the Church. However, the advantages of this procedure far outweighed the disadvantages because the entire approach could be individualized to correspond to the penitent's needs and also provided the guarantee of complete confidentiality.

Is there a way to combine the best of Penance's ancient tradition and the benefits of later developments? In our own day there have been attempts to do exactly this. The postconciliar rite of Penance provides for the option of communal celebrations of this sacrament, which help to recapture more vividly the communal sense of sin, repentance, and reconciliation. In such services all hear the Word of God proclaimed, acknowledge their sinfulness, individually confess their sins to a priest, and then receive the saving forgiveness of God (CCC 1482).

Our emotions in Penance should be genuine sorrow

and repentance, for we have sinned against God and one another (CCC 1451–53). But we should also feel hope because the Lord has given us the means to return to him. As God's people, and with confidence in our merciful Father, we approach this sacrament as a path to pardon, consolation, and joy.

If Jesus inaugurated his Resurrection appearances with the greeting of "Peace", we also know that he began his public ministry with the command: "Repent" (Mk 1:15). The Sacrament of Penance is the means by which Catholics go through the process of repentance, so as to experience Christ's peace (CCC 1431).

Or, as the confessor assures the penitent: "The Lord has freed you from your sins. Go in peace."

Some Difficulties in Regard to the Sacrament of Penance

In spite of the many positive values so apparent in the renewed rite and theology of Penance, one must admit that we have also come upon some difficulties with this sacrament over the past few decades. Theological questions or practical problems are not unique to the twentieth century; they are as old as the Church herself. Handled correctly, difficulties have always launched the

Church on a much deeper understanding of the matters under scrutiny. Four such concerns have developed in regard to the Sacrament of Penance.

Confessing to a Priest

The first issue is really perennial: "Why confess to a priest?" And what is at stake here is probably not so much the Sacrament of Penance as the Sacrament of Holy Orders. Divine forgiveness is not being questioned, but the need for a ministerial priesthood clearly is.

In the Judeo-Christian tradition, forgiveness has always been mediated. On Yom Kippur the Hebrew high priest spoke words of sorrow to the Lord on behalf of the whole people and then symbolically placed the year's sins on the head of a goat, driving him out of the community into the desert. Jesus consistently presented himself as an agent of divine forgiveness, so much so that some charged him with blasphemy (Lk 5:21). Nor did this mediatory role end with Christ; he clearly intended his apostles to stand in his stead vis-à-vis the Church and the world (cf. Jn 20:23; Lk 9:1; Mt 16:19; CCC 1461).

Christians are not rugged individualists; they come before the throne of mercy in the company of all the redeemed. Our relationship with God is personal, of course—but it is also communal. From a Catholic perspective, our personal relationship with God is enhanced by the communal and not diminished by it. The presence of a priest, as the ordained representative of Christ and the Church, is a concrete sign of both the communal and individual dimensions of a Christian's salvation. His presence is also a reminder that our sins not only offend the Lord but also his Mystical Body, the Church (CCC 1462).

On the level of human psychology, one can easily see the value of confessing to another person (CCC 1455). Every human being needs to "unload", to come to grips with personal guilt, and to receive guidance and encouragement. Most importantly, all people need to hear that they are indeed forgiven and to have that forgiveness celebrated in concrete, sacramental form.

Surely this insight is why other Christian bodies (for example, Episcopalians and Lutherans) have recently taken a second look at the Sacrament of Penance and decided to reintroduce this rite into their official liturgical life. Ecumenism can teach us to esteem more highly what we already possess by noticing what others are trying to rediscover.

Declining Numbers of Catholics Go to Confession

A second modern problem in regard to Penance is the decline in the numbers of people who use it. The usual response to this observation is: "I don't commit any mortal sins, Father; I don't have to go to confession." While it is true that the law of the Church requires sacramental confession once a year only if a Christian is conscious of having committed grave sin, this is a minimalist view of reality. The enthusiastic believer seeks to do the maximum, not the minimum.

Having heard confessions for many years now, I might agree that few people are guilty of truly grave sins, but I can also say with deep conviction that the best confessions I have heard have been those by people who are attentive to the "small" sins that offend our Lord. I am not speaking of scrupulosity but of sensitivity. As the saying goes, the greatest saints see themselves as the greatest sinners. We regard ourselves as good only because we tend to measure ourselves against some of the pagans among whom we live (and this is self-righteousness as well as a false comparison). We need to measure ourselves against the standard of Jesus Christ. When Peter saw himself in that light, he asked the Lord to leave him because he was such a sinful man (Lk 5:8). Frequent confession provides the impetus for perfection and offers the penitent the support needed for growth in holiness (CCC 1458).

General Absolution

During the past decades a third problem regarding Penance has been the misuse of "general absolution". This practice arose out of a misunderstanding or misapplication of the norms for communal penance services. Some priests and bishops assumed that simply because a large crowd appeared for the Sacrament of Penance and an insufficient number of priests were available, the conditions prevailed for the granting of general absolution without private confession of sins (as has always been done in combat situations).

This view was wrong on two scores. First, if general absolution is granted, the congregation must be told that the absolution is valid only if all mortal sins are confessed within the year and, further, that another general absolution may not be sought out until private confession has taken place. Second, general absolution was never envisioned as a normal alternative to private confession and, in fact, was intended to be most exceptional, involving extreme circumstances wherein penitents would have grave spiritual need without access to the sacrament for a prolonged period of time (CCC 1483). Such a situation is barely imaginable in the United States. Canon 961 of the Code of Canon Law and statements by Cardinal Joseph Ratzinger of the Sacred Congregation for the Doctrine of the Faith lend their weight to the position I have just outlined, as does the 1988 norm enacted by the United States Conference of Catholic Bishops.

Why did general absolution become so prevalent in some places? The unfortunate laxity of some priests, the desire of various liturgists and theologians to eliminate auricular confession, and the inclination of some people to take the easiest way out all combined to make this option so popular. For centuries Catholics have been accused of seeking "cheap grace"; the swiftness with which some Catholics responded to this deformation of Penance gave an ironic credibility to the charge.

It is strange that in an era when the cult of the individual is so strong, the Church should do away with one of her strongest signs of commitment to personalism and replace it with the anonymity of the crowd. Throughout Lent, John Paul II stresses repeatedly that the availability of private confession is a sign of Christ's love for each one of us as individuals, sacramentalized in the one-to-one encounter between priest and penitent. This revolutionary good news, so desperately needed today, is only obscured and confused by countersigns such as the improper use of general absolution.

First Penance

A final problem concerns the appropriate time for the celebration of First Penance. In the United States, experimentation with a delayed reception of Penance has occurred, so that a child received First Holy Communion in the second grade and then First Penance in perhaps the fourth grade or even later. The reason given for this change was that youngsters had grave difficulty in understanding sin and that a too-early reception of Penance could be psychologically harmful.

No objective data were ever offered to substantiate this approach, which was contrary to that practiced for centuries, and the experience of parents and teachers eventually bore out the validity of the traditional practice. If a child cannot understand the very human experience of sin, how can that same child comprehend the divine mystery of the Eucharist? On the psychological level, it is much less traumatic for a child of seven to confess a sin of disobedience as his first experience of Penance than for a high-schooler to have to confess fornication for a First Penance, as has happened.

This experiment was terminated years ago by direct order of the Holy See. Canon 914 of the revised Code makes this point very explicitly and with no qualifications. Thus, any parish that persists in delaying First Penance does so against the express will of the Church, God's people. Some observers have responded by saying that this is "forcing" a child to receive a sacrament, which is a violation of the child's rights and conscience. But that is unpersuasive.

The Church is the guardian of the sacraments, and she has the absolute right to determine the order in which the sacraments should be received. If a man decides he wants to be confirmed without having been baptized, is the Church "forcing" a sacrament on him by insisting that Baptism must precede Confirmation? Of course not. And so it is with First Penance and First Communion. The point is, children should never be pawns in the process of theological debate, especially where their salvation is concerned. And the Catholic Church teaches, quite clearly, that Penance should precede Eucharist.

Let us also remember one last point. Controversy is not always a bad thing, especially when it enables us to clarify our thinking on important issues. If we argue the issues Penance raises, it is because this sacrament is so important to us. And because we sense in it matters that have eternal consequences.

Questions for Group Discussion

1. What is the connection between the Risen Christ's gift of peace to the apostles and his institution of the Sacrament of Penance? How is that link maintained today?

2. What are the essential steps to take in making a good confession?

3. What is the meaning of the statement, "There is no such thing as a private sin"?

4. Why do Catholics confess their sins to a priest? How is private confession a sign of God's personal care in the Church?

5. Why do you think fewer people go to confession in our day? Discuss.

6

Matrimony

*"May Almighty God Bless You
by the Word of His Mouth and Unite Your Hearts
in an Enduring Bond of Love"*

THE MARRIAGE of two Christians was viewed by St. Paul as something deeply sacred because he saw in that relationship a direct parallel to the love of Christ for his Church (Eph 5:32; CCC 1617).

The love of a husband for his wife, then, must be unconditional. The husband's whole concern should be for the welfare of his wife, as hers should be for his. This is a high ideal, but Jesus expects us to be men and women of ideals. In fact, our purpose in life as Christians is to view human existence from a divine perspective, which is a theological way of saying that we must look on things the way God does.

Every marriage takes place, not in private, but in the presence of others, because it will profoundly affect the Church (CCC 1630, 1663). And each couple receives the support of the whole Christian community as they pledge the gift of themselves to one another because the act of self-giving is fundamental to Christian life (Jn 15:13).

The dignity of the married state comes from the love of the individuals committing themselves to each other and from the grace bestowed on the state by Christ himself (CCC 1601, 1613). Thus it is important to look upon a Christian marriage as an arena of salvation for the couple.

It is no accident that the Church of the West regards the bride and groom as the ministers of this sacrament (CCC 1623). They are the key agents of grace for each other. Having administered the sacrament to one another on their wedding day, they must continually provide each other with opportunities for growth in faith and love, to be Christ for each other. This is done most clearly in the unreserved, sacrificial gift of the self. And it is precisely here that so many couples fail. The old marriage rite reminded every couple that "sacrifice is usually difficult and irksome. Love can make it easy; perfect love can make it a joy." The quality of one's love is proven by the quality of one's giving (CCC 1601, 1609). Those factors determine whether or not a marriage is a genuine arena of salvation.

The Domestic Church

One of the great insights of Vatican II was the rediscovery of the Christian family as "the domestic Church". In other words, every Christian home should be a Church-in-miniature, for it is here that most people will begin to learn the basics of Christian life (CCC 1655–58, 1666).

The Code of Canon Law speaks of marriage as both a covenant and a contract. As a covenant, it must mirror God's relationship with the Chosen People and Christ's relationship with his Church. As a contract, it is the informed exchange of consent to accept the rights and duties of the marital state. These two views of marriage are not mutually exclusive but complementary. The realization that our Lord so loved his Church as to give his life for her should enable Christian spouses to be prepared to do the same.

It has been said that the Church must raise a prophetic voice in society. If that is true, then one might expect the "domestic Church" to offer a witness uniquely its own. However, many couples do not seem aware of their need to do this today, and we are the poorer for it. I would like to suggest some areas for such witness.

The Witness of Exclusivity
and Permanence

In the Christian scheme of things, the marital bond calls for exclusivity (CCC 1638, 1646-48). Here Catholic spouses have an especially powerful message to convey to a society in which soap operas and television melodramas glorify the notion of "open marriage", which is just a euphemism for infidelity. Christian couples must proclaim clearly and joyfully that total fidelity in marriage is God's will and, on that very account, meaningful. Conversely, they must argue persuasively that anything less than faithfulness can only cause heartache to the individuals involved and to society as a whole.

A Christian marriage is indissoluble: "Let no man separate what God has joined" (Mk 10:9; CCC 1611, 1614-16, 1643-45). Often we hear people say: "I don't agree with the Church's position on divorce and remarriage." To such people, committed Christian couples will say: "Please do not say, 'I disagree with the Church's position.' Better to say, 'I disagree with Christ's position.'" It will then be necessary to explain this "hard saying" of our Lord and to use the testimony of one's own married life to verify what God's grace can accomplish. Of course, God does not want his children to be miserable; but sometimes the greatest joys are experienced only after a couple has seen that divorce is not an option for genuine believers.

Love and Life Are Inextricably Linked

If marriage is truly a sign of God's love, it must be open to life (CCC 1652-54). The unitive and the procreative elements can never be separated. The unitive without the procreative is mere hedonism; the procreative without the unitive is mere reproduction of the species. Love and life are inextricably linked in the very nature of man and in the very nature of gender. A promiscuous society desperately needs to hear of normal, happily married Christians who do not find fulfillment in mere recreational sex. Contemporary culture longs to hear that one can and must love in a spirit of chastity. If Christian spouses are unwilling to say this, who else will?

"Marriage vs. celibacy" is the way life in the Church is sometimes depicted, and with some justification. However, a committed Christian couple and a committed Christian celibate are not in competition with each other (CCC 1618-20). Both forms of witness are valid and necessary. Both are sacraments or signs of higher realities. The bond of marriage is a reminder, in the present, of Christ's love for his Church. The life of celibacy points toward that future moment when God will be all in all. Catholic couples demonstrate in con-

crete, earthly ways the kind of sacrificial love that is at
the very heart of the gospel message. Celibate clergy
possess an objectivity in marital affairs that makes them
ideal marriage counselors; their own life of chastity
eminently qualifies them to serve as models of genuine
sacrificial love for their people and to challenge their
people to be all they can be, by cooperating with
divine grace. Catholic spouses, then, will refuse to become parties to that mentality which creates dichot-
omies where none exist or which holds that direct,
personal experience is required for a valid contribution to be made. On the contrary, they will un-
ashamedly declare their respect and love for their
priests, whose celibate lives enhance their own married lives.

More Than an Arrangement of Convenience

Catholic spouses are in a unique position to share the
Catholic mission of marriage. Their testimony is
needed not simply to justify or vindicate the Church's
point of view but to convince the world that marriage
is more than the arrangement of convenience it has
become so often in contemporary America. Catholic
couples must never conform to the ways of the world
but must do all in their power to transform the ways of
the world to those of Christ. Therein lies both the

difficulty and the nobility of the Christian vocation of marriage.

At every wedding the Church, through her knowledge of the past, helps couples gaze into their own uncertain future. In the final blessing of the old marriage rite, the Church summed up the essence of married life in poetic yet realistic form:

> May almighty God bless you by the Word of his mouth and unite your hearts in an enduring bond of pure love.
>
> May you be blessed in your children, and may the love you lavish on them be returned a hundredfold.
>
> May the peace of Christ dwell always in your hearts and in your home; may you have true friends to stand by you, both in joy and in sorrow. May you be ready with help and consolation for all those who come to you in need; and may the blessings promised to the compassionate descend in abundance on your home.
>
> May you be blessed in your work and enjoy its fruits. May care never cause you distress, nor the desire for earthly possessions lead you astray; but may your hearts' concern be always for the treasures laid up for you in the life of heaven.
>
> May the Lord grant you fullness of years, so that you may reap the harvest of a good life, and, after you have served him with loyalty in his kingdom on earth, may he take you up into his eternal dominions in heaven.

It is said that, unlike competitive games, marriage is a partnership in which both parties win or else both lose. A husband and wife are responsible for each other both in time and eternity; that is what the blessing means; that is what the Church's theology of marriage means; and that is what the grace of this special sacrament is meant to accomplish.

A Work of Justice, Not Mercy

When the Church uses her judicial system to examine the validity of a marriage bond, she is engaging in a work of justice and not a work of mercy. Both supporters and detractors of the revised annulment process seem to be confused in this regard. Therefore, some background information might be helpful (CCC 1629, 1601).

A decree of nullity (commonly but inaccurately referred to as an "annulment") is the Church's declaration that, after proper consideration, a determination has been made that the necessary qualities were lacking in one or both parties to the marriage, so that the *consortium totius vitae* (total sharing of a common life) envisioned by Vatican II was impossible.

In other words, what was taken to be a marriage was lacking in some essential characteristics. Simply put, no marriage really existed. This is quite different from a divorce, which is the declaration that a real marriage is now broken by some authority. Catholic theology, taking at face value the words of Christ in the Scriptures (cf. Mk 10:9), refuses to grant power to any human authority (civil or ecclesiastical) over a valid, consummated, sacramental marriage (CCC 1640).

After Vatican II the Holy See gave marriage tribunals in the United States permission to use special norms to handle annulment cases. This experimental process was apparently viewed quite favorably by Rome because, with a few exceptions, the process was incorporated into the revised Code of Canon Law and thus extended to the universal Church. Although critics can sometimes cite particular abuses (which should be promptly brought to the attention of the proper authorities), by and large the new norms have achieved justice in a way the old system could not.

It is important to note that having the Church's tribunal open to a Catholic is not a privilege but a right, flowing from one's membership in the Church. Therefore, Catholics can approach their parish priest with confidence regarding an annulment, or, if need be, they can consult with the judicial vicar of the diocese who is the chief judge of the local tribunal.

Some Particulars

The length of time and the fees involved in annulment cases vary significantly from diocese to diocese. Usually these differences are the result of whether a particular tribunal has sufficient staff (both priestly and secretarial). Although the media frequently try to show that an annulment is related to a petitioner's wealth or prestige, one must realize that the modest fees (sometimes as low as two hundred dollars) do not begin to cover the costs involved. Furthermore, it is extremely unlikely that any case has ever been denied because of the inability to pay. Incidentally, it is ironic how normally charitable Catholics can turn harsh when the rich or the famous obtain the same consideration as anyone else. Should justice be denied simply because these people are rich or famous?

The biggest difference between earlier annulment procedures and the present norms is the admissibility of psychological evidence. This was a direct response to Vatican II's call for the Church to be open to valid insights coming from the social sciences. Pope John Paul II has enthusiastically supported this approach and reminded the judges of the Roman Rota (the marriage court of the universal Church) of their obligation to take seriously such testimony, all the while calling for proper caution.

Grounds for Annulment

As the process begins, one must recall that the Church believes that marriage has the benefit of law, which is to say that the burden of proving invalidity is on the person requesting the decree of nullity. What are the grounds for such a decree? The first and easiest is "lack of form", which means the marriage ceremony did not take place according to the Church's requirements (CCC 1630–31); the second most common ground is "lack of due discretion" or lack of consent. Here is where the psychology of persons and marriage itself comes into play.

"Lack of discretion" refers to insufficient knowledge or reflection on the part of one or both spouses, to the degree that the marital consent given on the day of the ceremony was defective (CCC 1625–32). Full knowledge includes knowledge of the self, the other, and the demands of marriage. Adolescent fantasies do not produce Christian marriages, for example.

If one (or both) parties was unable to fulfill the obligations of marriage from the very beginning, no marriage ever took place (CCC 1629). True, spouses receive a special sacramental grace through Matrimony (CCC 1642), but theology also tells us that grace builds on nature. In other words, if the necessary prerequisites are not possessed by the spouses, no growth will ever occur. Immaturity, instability, dependency on drugs and alcohol, promiscuity—all are warning signals of potential marital problems. In reviewing a failed marriage, a petitioner should look for the presence of these indicators before the marriage ceremony took place. Information about one's early life, personal relationships, and life in the Church are critical, as are the details about the courtship, the honeymoon, and the marriage itself.

Finally, some clarifications are in order. According to Church law, neither divorce nor remarriage brings about an excommunication. However, someone who is divorced and remarried (civilly) cannot receive the Eucharist because the present relationship is one of adultery (CCC 1650–51). The solution to the problem is to investigate possibilities for an annulment and to refrain from conduct proper to marriage until such time as a decree of nullity would permit a Christian remarriage. Hard to do? Surely—and that is why our Lord's disciples concluded his views on marriage were so demanding that it might be better not to marry at all (Mt 19:10).

The correct conclusion to come to, of course, is not that marriage should be avoided but that it should be carefully prepared for (CCC 1632). This is a responsibility of the couple but also of the Church. It is to be hoped that extra care at this end of the marital spectrum will render unnecessary judicial proceedings at the other end.

Questions for Group Discussion

1. What is the meaning of the family as "the domestic Church"? What is the Christian family's special witness today?

2. What do the qualities of exclusivity and indissolubility in Christian marriage say about our views on God, man, and the Church?

3. How do marriage and celibacy complement each other in providing a Christian witness to the world?

4. How is Christian marriage rightly understood as a vocation?

5. What exactly is an annulment or a decree of nullity? What are some of the grounds for annulment?

7

Holy Orders

The Priest, an Icon of Jesus Christ,
Sacrifices His Own Life for the People's Sake

WHEN PEOPLE hear of "ordination", their thoughts generally turn to the priesthood, because that is their usual contact with the Sacrament of Holy Orders.

However, the sacrament actually involves three ministries: the diaconate, the priesthood, and the episcopacy (CCC 1536).

In all three orders, men are commissioned by a bishop's laying-on of hands (CCC 1538) to serve the Church by preaching God's Word "in season and out of season" (1 Tim 4:2) and by making present for God's people his saving mysteries.

A call to service in the Church comes from God and is acknowledged and validated by the Church. Like the prophets of the Old Testament and the apostles of the New Testament, once a man is consecrated by God for a special task, his ultimate meaning is bound up with that task (CCC 1583). If he relinquishes it, his own dignity and personal meaning, as well as that of the Church that calls him, are threatened. Surely that is the heart of our Lord's comment that one who puts his hand to the plow but keeps looking back is unfit for the kingdom (Lk 9:62).

Deacons

The diaconate, since Vatican II, has been restored to its original status as a distinct ministry (CCC 1571). For centuries the diaconate was regarded as a "stepping stone" to the priesthood. The Fathers of the Council, however, called for its restoration as a permanent state, especially for mission lands. This development has given rise to two categories of deacons: permanent (who usually have a secular occupation, are of a mature age, and may be married) and transitional (who are celibate and will become priests).

The liturgical functions of deacons include preaching, the distribution of Holy Communion, baptizing, and acting as the Church's official witness at marriage. The Acts of the Apostles indicates that their primary function was to do works of charity (6:1; CCC 1570).

It is interesting to note that some very reputable theologians, such as Louis Bouyer, question whether the diaconate truly belongs to the Sacrament of Orders. The rationale behind this line of argument comes from the fact that a deacon can do nothing after ordination that any layperson cannot do with proper delegation but without ordination. No dogmatic statement defines the diaconate as part of Orders; nonetheless, the general theological opinion and practice of the Church would hold for its inclusion.

Priests

The priesthood exists for the Eucharist (CCC 1566). This was certainly the mind of Christ as he instituted these two sacraments within the context of the Passover Supper (Lk 22:17-20). Fidelity to the Lord's command requires the continued celebration of the Eucharist, which, in turn, requires a ministerial priesthood. Having said that, we must face up to the fact that the New Testament never speaks of the apostles or their successors as priests. Why so?

The first and most obvious reason was a fear that Christian ministers would be identified with either the Jewish or pagan priesthoods, and the early Church felt a strong need to distance herself from both. The second reason was a concern that the unique high priesthood of Jesus Christ not be clouded over (Heb 8; CCC 1544-45). Just as Christ's redemptive sacrifice was effected once and for all (never to be repeated), so too is Christ's priesthood unique. However, the

Eucharist, which sacramentally re-presents the Sacrifice of Calvary, requires priestly ministers. Such ministers are not priests in their own right but participate in the priesthood of Jesus Christ. This point is sometimes lost on certain other Christians who think the Catholic notion of priesthood in some way nullifies the unique priesthood of Jesus.

The New Testament is also quite clear in describing the entire community of the Church as a "royal priesthood" (1 Pet 2:9; CCC 1546). If so, why a priestly "caste" within the Church? The Hebrew Scriptures spoke of the Israelites as a royal priesthood (cf. Ex 19:6), but they still had a priestly class. If the Israelite community as a whole was to fulfill its priestly witness in the world, it needed the ministry of priests. The Church is no different: Having been ministered to by their priests, the people can then minister to the world (CCC 1547).

No competition should exist between clergy and laity because all Christians are called to serve both Christ and the world. It is not a question of who is better but merely of different ways to serve. It is ironic that, despite our contemporary understanding of sociology and psychology, we should experience so much role confusion as some clergy seek to run for public office and some laity seek to administer the sacraments. This situation is a result of poor self-understanding on the part of both clergy and laity. A careful reflection on

Paul's theology of the Body of Christ might be very profitable (1 Cor 12).

The Tradition of Priestly Celibacy

An ancient tradition of the Latin rite calls for celibate priests (CCC 1579). The priest's concern for the Church must be total, so that his individual attention and love are centered on his ministry (cf. 1 Cor 7). However, some misunderstandings about celibacy need to be clarified. First, celibacy does not depreciate marriage; its place in the priesthood emphasizes the fact that marriage and priesthood are vocations in themselves and that both deserve one's complete commitment (CCC 1620).

Second, the reasons behind celibacy are not simply pragmatic, for example, greater priestly availability or economy. Celibacy is meant to be an eschatological sign that reminds people that "we have here no lasting city" and that our sights need to be set on that city "where God is all in all". The witness of celibacy for the sake of the kingdom is all the more needed today precisely because we live in such a sex-saturated society.

Third, the ecclesiastical law of priestly celibacy is not divine in origin, although surely the Lord's clear preference (cf. Mt 19:29; Lk 14:26). This means that the law does admit of exceptions. For this reason, the Holy See has granted special permission for some married Anglican clergy who have joined the Roman Catholic Church to maintain their marital and family commitments and also to be admitted to the priesthood.

The Specific Functions of a Priest

A priest is a witness to the gospel and a proclaimer of the gospel (CCC 1564-66). That Word then needs to take on flesh. Hence, a priest is ordained for two specific functions: to offer the Sacrifice of the Mass and to be an agent of reconciliation in the Sacrament of Penance. A priest must also do more than this. He must truly be a father to his people, standing as a constant sign of dedication to the gospel and to reflecting the mercy of Christ.

It is for this very reason that Catholics have always devotedly returned their priests' love by calling them "Father". Cardinal John Henry Newman observed that, of all the titles he had held in his life, that of "Father" meant the most to him. This title should not create distance between priest and people but should serve as a reminder of the depth of the relationship that exists—a relationship that is essentially familial. Nor are critics on solid scriptural ground who question this usage based on Matthew 23:9. The clear intent of this passage is to forbid giving to any human being the honor due God himself. The same critics usually see no difficulty in addressing their male parents as "father" or in referring to physicians, professors, and ministers as "doctor" (teacher), a title likewise mentioned in the Matthean passage.

Bishop

A bishop possesses the fullness of the priesthood (CCC 1557–59). As such, he is the chief priest of his diocese and is capable of administering all the sacraments. He serves as a symbol of unity and continuity; a bishop provides the link with the apostolic Church. His teaching authority rests on that fact and on his union with the entire college of bishops under the headship of the Pope.

I am writing these reflections about Holy Orders on the eve of my own anniversary of priestly ordination. At this time each year I make a special point of thanking God for giving the Church the gift of the priesthood and for my vocation. Because a priest deals with intangible realities, it is often hard for him to calculate his own effectiveness. Most priests will never know the tremendous good they have done. Perhaps that is one reason some priests hesitate to invite other young men to join their ranks. The solution to the so-called vocations crisis lies in a rediscovery of the meaning of this sacred ministry in the Church.

Or, as a French spiritual writer said: "If people

could realize what the priesthood is, there would be too many priests."

Wait a Minute, Why Only Men?

If it is true that the priesthood exists for the Church and the Eucharist, then it is entirely appropriate for us to reflect on one of today's most controversial questions: "Why only male priests?"

Of course, honesty requires us to note that the ordination of women is, for the most part, an issue only in the United States, Canada, and portions of Western Europe. It is also rather predictably derived from the secular feminist movement.

Both of these observations should give us reason to pause. Proponents of women's ordination maintain that the Church has no clearly articulated theology on this matter. Thus they come to the conclusion that this teaching is based on sexual prejudice. On the former point we might agree, but not on the latter.

A detailed explanation of the "male-only priesthood" does not exist, and with good reason. It has never before been a point of contention. The Church rarely works out a full-blown theology until it is called for by the circumstances of the times. Thus the Church always believed in and taught the doctrine of the two natures of Christ. However, until the doctrine was attacked, definitive formulations were not brought forth. The clear statement of the hypostatic union was achieved at the Council of Chalcedon as a response to the Monophysite heresy.

Arguments against the Ordination of Women

In the current debate, we should realize that the burden of proof rests on those seeking to change tradition. This is standard debate procedure and one not adhered to by many of the partisans of women's ordination. The best argument against the ordination of women is really the simplest but also the most easily caricatured: It has never been done. No other issue resulting from the Second Vatican Council so clearly flies in the face of tradition; a vernacular liturgy, permanent deacons, and even married priests all find precedent in tradition.

The Holy Father has consistently said that the Church cannot ordain women (CCC 1577); not that she also does not want to do it, just that she does not have the power to do so. The reason is that Jesus Christ, Lord of the Church, chose only men. "But Christ was limited by his own culture, which had a low opinion of women", comes the retort. That might be true, at least in the sense that our Lord had to preach the gospel to a people who were limited by their own cultural conditioning. However, Jesus never hesitated to break with other cultural patterns of his day (for example, dining with sinners). How do we explain this apparent inconsistency, except to say that the all-male apostolic ministry is an expression of divine will?

Second, it is important to recognize that in the Christian faith sexuality is not a matter of indifference, for Christianity is an incarnational religion that takes the flesh seriously. In the early Church the Gnostic sects tried to say that sexual differences did not matter; the reader will recall that the Gnostics had problems accepting the humanity of Christ. The Church responded by asserting the symbolic value of the flesh as well as its real meaning as part of God's creation. In the Christian scheme of things, neither sex is *better* than the other. Each is *different* from the other.

Third, the reasons for a male priesthood are enhanced by Byzantine theology. When God chose to reveal himself, he did so through the taking on of human flesh by the second Person of the Blessed Trinity as God's Son. Anyone called to the priesthood since is called as a member of the one and unique priesthood of Jesus Christ. Just as Jesus was the icon (image) of the Father, so is the priest to be an icon of Jesus. This is also tied in with the so-called scandal of particularity, which reminds us that God's ways are not our ways. For example, why did God call the Jews and not the

Romans or the Greeks, who were certainly better educated and far more cultured? We do not know. Nor do we know why men are chosen as instruments of sacramental grace, especially since the qualities they are expected to show forth in their lives are often looked upon as "feminine" virtues (such as patience, humility, kindness). Perhaps the paradox itself contains the answer: God chooses whomever he wills to confound our human expectations and to show what an incredible new order of reality is being established. We must be comfortable in living with mystery.

Fourth, we are not dealing with a question of rights here, for no one (male or female) has a "right" to ordination (CCC 1578). If persons had such a right, the Church would not be able to set any prerequisites for Orders in regard to health or intelligence or moral living. All that would be necessary would be the assertion of a self-perceived inner call. No, a call to priesthood is one that comes from the Church and not from the individual. The biggest problem of all, however, is the strange idea that somehow sacramental ordination increases one's holiness or one's chances for salvation. Neither logic nor experience bears this out. Far from a question of rights, then, it is really a question of a diversity of roles and ministries in the Church—all of which are needed for the building up of the Body of Christ. In the natural order a man should not feel inferior to a woman simply because he is incapable of bearing children. His role is different, and so it is in the Church.

Finally, we must remember that the role of a priest in the liturgy is to stand in the person of Christ (the icon of the Father), not as part of the people, but as their head (CCC 1548, 1563; cf. CCC 1553). In the liturgy we witness a union between the bride (the Church) and the groom (Christ). That spousal union is made visible and sacramental through a male priesthood—and only through a male priesthood.

Questions for Group Discussion

1. How do the ministerial priesthood and the priesthood of the faithful complement each other in building up the Church?

2. For what specific purposes are men ordained? Discuss.

3. How does the ministerial priesthood participate in the priesthood of Jesus Christ? Does it detract from the uniqueness of Christ's priesthood in any way?

4. What is the usual role of a permanent deacon in a parish today?

5. What does it mean when we speak of a bishop having "the fullness" of the Sacrament of Holy Orders?

6. Obtain a copy of Pope John Paul II's *Ordinatio sacerdotalis*, as well as the subsequent clarification

offered by the Congregation for the Doctrine of the Faith. What do these two documents add to the discussion of the ordination of women?

8

Anointing of the Sick

*By Our Own Suffering We Share in the Mission
of Christ, a Mission That Redeems the World*

O F ALL THE sacraments, the Anointing of the Sick
is probably the least understood.

A good indication of this is the fact that its name has
been changed so often: Extreme Unction, Anointing
of the Sick. In common parlance it even took on "Last
Rites".

With each subsequent name change, the Church
has tried to clarify the purpose of this sacrament. Most
of us grew up with "Extreme Unction" (last anointing; CCC 1512), and surely this did not help produce
a healthy understanding of the sacrament.

However, even since Vatican II, fears and misunderstandings have persisted. Most people, for example, still
regard this sacrament as intended only for those on
their deathbed. But nothing could be further from the
mind of the Church. Anyone who is seriously ill is

eligible (CCC 1514–15). And in cases of old age, almost any illness takes on a serious nature. Moreover, the rite may be repeated, even in the course of the same sickness, if the patient suffers a relapse or the condition worsens. (The deceased should not be anointed, of course—since sacraments can be received only by the living—but the priest should recite prayers for the repose of the soul and be present to console the family.)

At the same time, it must be noted that the sacrament should not be administered for frivolous reasons.

The Sacrament's Purpose

What, then, is the purpose of the Anointing of the Sick? God is with his people, through the Church's sacraments, at every significant juncture of their lives. This sacrament is the Church's way of being present to a sick member, expressing the concern of the community and praying for this particular Christian's recovery. Since this person has been a faithful member of the Church throughout his life, the Church now comes to him with words of consolation, healing, and hope in imitation of the Lord Jesus during his earthly life and ministry.

The rite is very biblical in its theology and origins. In his work of healing, Jesus not only cured physical ills but also forgave men's sins (CCC 1503). In the prayer of anointing, this connection between physical and spiritual illness is clearly made: "Through this holy anointing may the Lord in his love and mercy help you with the grace of the Holy Spirit. May the Lord who frees you from sin save you and raise you up" (CCC 1513).

In this way, the Church continues Christ's ministry of healing and forgiveness. Biblical theology has always linked sin and sickness in such a way that sickness was seen as an effect of sin, not necessarily personal, but surely the result of sin in the world. Because this sacrament is as concerned with spiritual wholeness as it is with physical wholeness, a priest is its minister (CCC 1516).

Biblical theology has also emphasized the unity of body and soul, so that the human person is seen as a whole person and not compartmentalized or dissected as if for investigation under a microscope. Restoration to wholeness is the goal of this sacrament, beautifully symbolized by the anointing, the prayer of faith, and the laying on of hands—in fidelity to the rite described in James 5:14–16 (CCC 1519, 1531). Vatican II's *Lumen gentium* expresses the rationale for the sacrament in this way: "By the sacred anointing of the sick and the prayer of the priests, the whole Church commends those who are ill to the suffering and glorified Lord that he may raise them up and save them."

This idea of the activity of "the whole Church" represents the recovery of a wonderful notion that was gradually lost over the centuries. In the renewed sacrament, the sick person sees himself as part of the entire community of faith, who pray for him, and never as isolated from the Church (CCC 1517, 1522). This communal dimension is highlighted in two ways. First, the option now exists that allows the celebration of this sacrament for an entire group of sick people. Second, even when only one person receives the sacrament, the new rite stresses the fact that the care of the sick is the work not only of priests but of all Christians.

As the priest attends to the sacramental needs of the ailing, all the members of the Church need to be involved on their behalf by visiting the sick, helping them in any way possible, and praying with them and for them. Furthermore, the rite also emphasizes the communal dimension of this sacrament by inviting family, friends, and neighbors to participate.

Last Rites

Sometimes the Anointing of the Sick is indeed part of a broader ceremony, correctly known as Last Rites (CCC 1524–25). Here the person is dying and is assisted in his last moments by the Church's sacramental system: confession, anointing, Viaticum (food for the journey), blessing. Again, family and friends should be encouraged to be present to stand in solidarity with this believer who is preparing for that meeting with Christ for which he lived his whole life.

The Role of Suffering in the Christian's Life

No discussion of the Anointing of the Sick would be complete without some consideration of the question of suffering (CCC 1500–1501), which every human being must face. A person has only two choices in the face of suffering: to shrink from it and become bitter, or to embrace it and grow as a result. A Christian never looks for pain or sickness. In fact, he does everything possible to overcome such negative experiences, following the example of Christ himself, who could pray, "Father, if it is your will, take this cup from me" (Lk 22:42). But the believer will also continue to echo our Lord yet more, as he adds: "Yet not my will but yours be done."

Suffering has redemptive value for the individual, for the Church, and for the world (CCC 1505). The realization that God sends the biggest crosses to those he loves prompted Teresa of Avila to observe half-jokingly, half-seriously, "If that is the way you treat your friends, Lord, it's no wonder you have so few of them."

It is the task of the Church, and especially of the priest who ministers to the sick, to help them see in their sufferings a loving Father; to see that through their sufferings, they are sharing in the sufferings of Christ (CCC 1521); to see beyond their suffering to the joy of the Resurrection (cf. Rom 6:5). This can happen only when the sick are reconciled to the divine will, relinquishing secular notions of happiness and fulfillment.

The Holy Father's apostolic letter *Salvifici doloris* makes a truly wonderful contribution to the Christian theology of the Cross and can be read by both the well and the sick to great personal profit. Cardinal Terence Cooke, in the last days of his life, spoke convincingly about the meaning of human existence and cautioned against a "quality of life" ethic that would devalue suffering: "Life is no less beautiful when it is accompanied by illness or weakness, hunger or poverty, physical or mental diseases, loneliness or old age."

Adopting that philosophy of life enables a Christian to put his suffering to good use by uniting it to that of the Crucified One who thus redeemed the world (CCC 1505). As Catholic children growing up, we were told so often to "offer up" our little aches and pains. The Sisters were encouraging us to put our suffering to good use. How wise they were!

Lumen gentium says that the Church "exhorts [the sick] to contribute to the good of the people of God by freely uniting themselves to the passion and death of Christ." In my own ministry to the sick, I have seen how valuable an awareness of redemptive suffering can be, spiritually, psychologically, and sometimes even physically.

I always ask the sick to "offer up" their suffering for religious vocations or the intentions of the Holy Father. This forces them to focus on some reality outside themselves and to see themselves as making a contribution to the good of souls even on their sickbeds. Illness, then, does not diminish their participation in the Mystical Body of Christ. Rather, it enhances it (CCC 1508).

Because the Church is a good mother, she is with her children both in joy and in sorrow. She is with her sons and daughters in the joy of Baptism or Matrimony or Holy Orders. She is with us to sustain us in Penance and the Eucharist. She is with us in our times of trouble and weakness and "at the hour of our death".

By introducing us to Christ in the sacraments, she prepares us to meet the Lord in judgment. If we have learned well, we shall not hesitate to say in our final moments, with eagerness and longing, "Come, Lord Jesus" (Rev 22:20). To which he will respond: "Yes, I am coming soon!"

Questions for Group Discussion

1. What is the biblical understanding of the connection between sin and physical illness?
2. Why do you suppose the Church reestablished communal rites of anointing? Why have they become so popular?
3. Discuss, in detail, the redemptive value of suffering.
4. What is the difference between the Sacrament of the Anointing of the Sick and the Last Rites?

Epilogue

"A Baker's Dozen of Obstacles"

W E HAVE BEEN studying the sacraments and their place in Catholic life. To conclude, it might be a good idea to identify those elements of personal or communal life that keep us from appreciating in all their fullness these avenues of grace and holiness. I have assembled what I have termed "a baker's dozen of obstacles to an appreciation of the sacraments". I have not arranged them in any special priority order and, regrettably, the list is not exhaustive. But let us consider each of them.

1. The Lack of Eschatology

"Eschatology" is an intimidating word for a most essential aspect of Christian faith, namely, conviction about the afterlife. Sacraments, you see, ultimately make no sense if we do not view our life here below as

"A Baker's Dozen of Obstacles to an Appreciation of the Sacraments" was an address delivered on the occasion of the Peoria Diocesan Summer Institute, June 6–8, 1996, at Bradley University.

the prelude to something bigger, better, and more enduring. Cardinal Ratzinger maintains that the gravest
error of the postconciliar period has been the shunting
off of eschatology to the sidelines of the Catholic experience. Admittedly, forty years ago one could get the
impression that life on earth was little more than a
troublesome way station through which we had to pass
to get to the "real thing". But we've now gone to the
other extreme in many cases, both in our preaching
and in our teaching. Twenty years ago, people were
already remarking that one never heard homilies on
hell anymore; now, it is hard to discover homilies on
heaven, except from some silly but well-meaning
priests who canonize every body brought into the
center aisle of their churches for a funeral—you know,
even as the widow sits there wondering if the homilist
could be talking about the man she knew!

Seriously, though, we must get back to a balanced
notion of how the present fits into the future; we must
strike the happy medium that loves life to the full, all
the while being able to nod in agreement to the conviction of the author of the Epistle to the Hebrews:
"For here we have no lasting city, but we seek the city
which is to come" (Heb 13:14). The sacraments are the
meeting place between time and eternity, between
heaven and earth; hence, a one-dimensional view of
things does irreparable damage to the sacramental system as God willed it for our salvation. Sacramentality

without eschatology is meaningless and ineffectual sentimentality.

2. A Misreading of *Sacrosanctum Concilium*

Please do not think me irreverent when I say that the greatest Catholic secret is not the "third secret of Fatima". Without fear of contradiction, I believe it is the material contained in Vatican II's *Sacrosanctum concilium*, with the *General Instruction of the Roman Missal* giving it competition for the most neglected. Before anyone is allowed to declare something a desideratum of the Council, it should have to be proved that the person in question has indeed read the *Constitution on the Sacred Liturgy*—and has read it with the same lenses as the Council Fathers who approved it. A careful reading of that text reveals that the goal was to be liturgical renewal, not a liturgical reform that has devolved into liturgical choreography, which, in turn, has led to little more than an incessant rearranging of the deck chairs on the Titanic.

Some may remember Father C. J. McNaspy's book entitled *Change, Not Changes*. In other words, what the Council had in mind was enabling us to engage in an interior conversion, so that we could approach worship with minds and hearts renewed; only then would incidentals make any sense. Instead, especially in the United States, we have been made to think that the heart and soul of the liturgical movement was adding and deleting prayers or moving furniture and persons around the sanctuary. That idea is both superficial and wrong, and no justification for it can be found in *Sacrosanctum concilium*; if anything, the document condemns such a view: "[T]here must be no innovations unless the good of the Church genuinely and certainly requires them, and care must be taken that any new forms adopted should in some way grow organically from forms already existing" (no. 23).

3. Spiritualism/Neo-Gnosticism

Through signs and symbols, the created, visible world brings us into contact with the uncreated, invisible world. Ironically, not a few liturgists who press mightily for a deeper appreciation of sign and symbol are the gravest offenders when it comes to what I dub "neo-gnosticism". The "old" gnostics had no use for the material universe and so despised the use of sacramental signs. Their contemporary descendants do not see how important it is to take symbols seriously—which means, among other things, not tampering with them unnecessarily.

As the priest-sociologist Andrew Greeley is fond of saying, "When you're talking about a symbol, you can never modify it by the adverb 'just'." Nothing is "just a symbol". As a body-soul unity, man needs signs and symbols to direct and focus his being on affairs outside the normal scope or range. When people sneer at the attachment of the faithful to certain forms of worship, we are face-to-face with a cynical intellectualism run amok. St. Thomas Aquinas understood man well when he asserted that "we arrive at the invisible through the visible."

4. Exaggerated Immanentism

One of the more tragic developments in liturgy has been an anthropocentrism that has pitted itself, with a vengeance, against theocentrism, that is, an approach to liturgy that has so emphasized the horizontal as to obfuscate or even, in some instances, obliterate the vertical. Now, no one would be foolish enough to suggest that human considerations and realities should not be given due attention in the celebration of worship; after all, as Pope John Paul has put it so well, "man cannot live without adoring." So, yes, there must be concern for what "makes us tick", so that worship can be "meaningful" in the most profound way we can interpret that word. However, the focus must none-theless be clear: It is God Whom we must adore, not ourselves. How many times we have read or heard: The liturgy is a celebration of ourselves—who we are, as persons and as a community. There is a truth there, but it is "out of sync". The imbalance reminds me of a freshman boy in high school who decides that he wants to become another Arnold Schwartzenegger: He works out day after day, with such concentration on his chest that no other part of the body is attended to. As a result, within a few months he has a 45-inch chest but spindly legs and no biceps or abdominal muscles to speak of. And our reaction? The sight is silly at best and grotesque at worst!

In much the same way, when we lose sight of the sacred and the transcendent, we distort the nature of Christian worship so fundamentally as to make it of little use, in the end, to man and an abomination to God. We desperately need to recapture reverence, awe, and mystery in our rites; without those basic components, it is no surprise that our young people inform us that they find the liturgy "boring". Believe it or not, they are not thereby saying that they want to be entertained—inviting us to bring on the clowns and the dancing girls; on the contrary, they are saying they want—and need—to be uplifted. How else to explain their fascination with various cults or even their rather improbable attraction to Gregorian chant CD's? As G. K. Chesterton put it, "The world will not starve for want of wonders, but only for want of wonder."

5. A Lost Sense of Sin

If we have lost our sense of the sacred, even more have we lost our sense of sin, so much so that more than two decades ago, the non-believing psychiatrist Karl Menninger could author a book entitled *Whatever Became of Sin?* Granted, we Catholics are not Lutherans or Calvinists or Fundamentalists, who almost delight in sin. But we must take account of sin—it has been an indispensable element of the human equation since the sin of our first parents. In fact, the ever-quotable Chesterton once quipped that the only dogma of the Catholic faith that is absolutely provable from human experience is original sin. And it is precisely because of the existence of sin and our weak human natures that God, in his goodness, gave us the sacramental system. Adam and Eve, in the state of original justice, did not need sacraments; they communicated with God face-to-face.

Therefore, any effort to diminish the sad truth about man as a sinner brings in its wake an even sadder fact of life, and that is the fact that the alienation between God and the individual then becomes much more acute and the alienation within the self that much more intolerable. Any good psychologist will tell you that denial is a most unhealthy defense mechanism. Only when we confront the bad news of human sinfulness can we latch onto the good news of salvation in and through

Jesus Christ. Those who have taught primary school children to read know that, whether the teacher calls the reading groups blue birds or cardinals or sparrows, the poor readers know who they are—and euphemisms or outright disavowal of real differences only makes things worse—for the overall educational process and especially for the children themselves. Similarly, we must recall that each and every sacrament is, in some way, connected to returning man to his lost innocence. And that awareness should make us rejoice in the goodness of God and in the nearness of our salvation. Anything less is but a shadow of the fullness and brightness of the whole truth.

6. Excessive Subjectivity

In the "old days", it is probably fair to say, the sacramental principle of *ex opere operato* may have been overemphasized, but now that is being done with the companion principle of *ex opere operantis*. What do I mean? When the Church affirms that the sacraments act *ex opere operato*, this means that they "work" simply by virtue of the power of Christ's grace, so that with a duly ordained minister, proper form and matter, and a right intention, a sacrament is valid (CCC 1128). This reminds us—in a powerful way—that Christ is the principal celebrant of every sacrament and that his grace is sovereign. That truth should be most consoling and reassuring to us for any number of reasons, but it can lead to some unfortunate developments, such as many of us witnessed in the preconciliar liturgical experience of the Church: a desiccated formalism and minimalism that all too often asked only what was needed for validity, thus deeming everything else "icing on the cake". And so, we often found rushed, mumbled prayers, hasty gestures, irreverent attitudes, and unprepared homilies.

Nowadays, we suffer from the flipside. The teaching *ex opere operantis* holds that human cooperation is needed in order for the offer of divine grace to be fruitful. And that has brought about a new form of Pelagianism. Pelagius, in the fifth century, preached the sufficiency of human effort for salvation; he was mightily resisted by none other than one of the greatest Fathers of the Church, St. Augustine. The Doctor of Grace acknowledged that, to be sure, there is a human element to man's salvation, but he stressed that God's work is primary and indispensable. In much of the liturgical practice of the day, we encounter both implicit and explicit denials of the necessity of grace. In all too many of the ICEL translations, for example, the Latin word *gratia* is totally ignored in the English renditions. Liturgists who resort to gimmicks smacking of manipulation of both God and man are concrete indicators of this phenomenon. Switching the focus in Confirmation from God's gracious gift of himself to strengthen us in our battle against the world, the flesh, and the devil to one of a "personal choice" or an "adult decision" is a good example of what I am talking about.

Catholic truth always takes account of the adage: *In medio stat virtus.* Therefore, *ex opere operato* because Jesus said, "without me, you can do nothing" (Jn 5:5). But also and equally, *ex opere operantis* because, as St. Augustine put it so beautifully, "The God who created us without us will not save us without us." Our liturgical praxis must keep those two sides of the one truth in a creative and positive tension.

7. The Reduction of Language, Art, and Music to the Least Common Denominator

Thomas Day tweaked the members of the liturgical establishment with his insightful and popular book *Where Have You Gone, Michelangelo?* The sign of their discomfort was their near-total silence in response. So much of the external dimension of Catholic worship in the postconciliar period is impoverished, banal, and bleak. A visitor from Mars would never imagine that we are supposed to be the spiritual descendants of a Giotto or Vivaldi, a Da Vinci or Vittoria, a Boromini or Palestrina. Style and class have been banished from most Catholic sanctuaries in our land—and we are all the poorer for it. The transient, the ephemeral, the cheap have replaced the beautiful, the uplifting, the inspiring. The perfect symbol of all this is the disposable missalette, for there is little of permanence to be found therein.

When we survey the landscape of the would-be liturgical arts of the past thirty-five years, what do we behold? Truth be told, we find little, except for what was created last year or the year before. Think about it: When did you last hear "Kumbaya" or "Sons of God" (even allowing for its "sexist" title!)? Has there been any artwork that anyone will want to preserve into the next millennium, let alone look at? What do ugly vestments that resemble horse blankets do for a person's aesthetical sense? Have you ever wondered what became of the clay and pottery vessels of the sixties, and why we should think their glass or crystal substitutes of the eighties will be any more enduring?

As we turn our gaze toward the language of worship, what could be more confusing and upsetting than English translations that are of a lower quality than most tabloids and of dubious theological worth? Only a fool would imagine that the average worshipping Catholic on any given Sunday morning is a Shakespearean scholar, but he is not an idiot, either. The genius of the *Book of Common Prayer* was that it used elevated language to elevate an entire nation, so that words, phrases, and thought patterns of that liturgical text became the very fiber of language of the English people from that day forward. Aside from the theological value of translating "*et cum spiritu tuo*" as "and with your spirit", who can deny the incredible graciousness of it as an alternative to the crude, crass, and abrupt, "and also with you"?

We are not faced only with a question of taste, so that the whole discussion can be dismissed with a wave of the hand and the adage "*De gustibus non est disputandum*." Far from it. Eamon Duffy has shown from history, in his *Stripping of the Altars*, how the liturgical terrorists of the English Reformation saw their barbarisms as a necessary element of their overall program, which was not really reform but revolution. Forewarned is forearmed.

Please do not get me wrong. I am not arguing for a "bells and smells" attitude in regard to liturgy, so well exemplified by the Anglicans, because, in sadness, we must admit that most of them are "all dressed up with nowhere to go". But once again, there is a happy medium between foppishness and the contemporary cult of the slob. Beyond that, it is crucial to recall that Aristotle taught us that "the good, the true, and the beautiful" coinhere, that is, you cannot have one without the other. Having lost the beautiful, should we be amazed to wake up and find that we have eventually lost the good and the true as well?

8. Celebration of Sacraments without Requisite Faith or Knowledge

Someone has observed that the contemporary problem may be summed up in the line that all too many of our people are "sacramentalized but not catechized". I would go yet a step farther and say that in many instances they are not even evangelized. Granted, we believe that sacraments confer grace by their very operation, but *Sacrosanctum concilium*, which spends several paragraphs talking about this matter, makes the point that all this presupposes recipients who are "well-disposed" (SC, nos. 59–61). In addition to the obvious element of being in the state of grace, proper disposition includes faith and a basic grasp of the doctrines involved. Without those two dimensions, the Church's sacramental life would be little more than magic—a caricature of her teaching and tradition from time immemorial.

In its modern garb, this phenomenon has often taken on the form of so-called "community-building rituals", so that the spiritual significance of the sacraments has been eviscerated and replaced with nothing more than a communal, humanistic dimension. How critical, then, it is to ensure that children and adults alike are brought to an explicit faith in the mysteries we celebrate and receive strong, on-going formation in the nature of these saving rites. Experiential, affective aspects must always be grounded in objective, theological truths. In my priestly ministry, not uncommonly I look out onto a congregation of predominantly blank stares, signalling a lack of awareness of what is happening; this is especially true at weddings, baptisms, funerals, first communions, and confirmations—but increasingly so at the Sunday Eucharist—all of which suggests that faith and/or knowledge are missing. Priests and catechists must address this problem in a unified manner, inasmuch as we have already lost most of two generations and now many who once believed and knew are also losing their moorings.

9. American Pragmatism

We Americans are notorious for being satisfied with the "quick fix", which leads to a poor sense of liturgy and is revealed in minimalism. The old "get 'em in and get 'em out" mentality did not die with the last celebration of the preconciliar rites. We find it today when people ask questions like: Is incense *required*? If not, forget it. It is operative when pastors decide that they will use extraordinary ministers of Holy Communion "because otherwise it will take too long". It comes to the fore when we go for a vessel or vestment that is ugly and cheap because it "works" just as well as something beautiful and more expensive.

We need to recapture the idea of liturgy as having

no practical purpose—only to adore God and elevate man. More than two decades ago, Hugo Rahner wrote a book called *Man at Play*. Father Rahner used the expression in its best and most profound sense, namely, that the most important thing man can do is to "waste" time and energy before his God. In this context, it is also worth recalling that someone as devoted to holy poverty as St. Francis could say that while his friars would wear rags, the vessels and vestments associated with the altar would always be of the finest quality. Mary Magdalen teaches us a valuable lesson in her lavish behavior toward the Lord, who, it must be remembered, praised her generous abandon. I believe it is also important to appropriate the Eastern concept of liturgy as something done "outside time". In practice, that would eliminate clock-watching or the intrusion of "worldly" things; not by accident, the Liturgy of the Eucharist of the Byzantine Rite begins with a hymn in which the faithful pray for the ability to put aside "all earthly cares". This is not escapism; it is acknowledging that love demands one's full attention to be focused on the Beloved.

10. "Monkey" Bishops/Liturgy Offices

By this term, I refer to those in authority who are committed to hearing, seeing, and speaking no evil. In other words, they don't want to be confronted by reality and do not wish to confront it, either. Therefore, when liturgical abuses are reported, they are ignored or glossed over or, worse yet, the complainer is labeled "negative" or "legalistic". I am firmly convinced that demands for the Tridentine Mass are directly related to the inability of those in authority to control the celebration of the sacred liturgy according to the revised rites. Many indult-Mass devotees mistakenly equate the new rite with aberrations, forgetting that, without enforcement of norms, the old rite would go in exactly the same direction. After all, if a priest or other minister has no intention of following the rubrics and his superior has no intention of making him do so, were a liturgy handwritten by the Son of God himself, it would be ruined as well.

But another disturbing pattern has emerged in this regard over the past thirty years, and that is what I have dubbed "rewarding disobedience". Three examples stand out: Communion-in-the-hand, Communion from the chalice on Sundays, and altar girls. Now, regardless of what you think of any or all of these developments, one must admit that all three were strictly forbidden and only by gross disobedience were they perpetrated; but the worst part of it all was that eventually authorities caved into the pressure and "legalized" the practices. No matter how you slice the cake, this is the recipe for liturgical chaos. I am put in mind of a young priest who insisted on celebrating

Mass facing east and was told by the diocesan office of worship he could not do it (even though the rubrics do presume every priest is facing east); he continued and was finally called in by the bishop and ordered to cease. He told the bishop he intended to go on as usual and that he was sure the old way of celebrating Mass was going to return imminently and he was just preparing his people for the change. He sealed his argument with the line, "You know, Bishop, the way you encouraged altar girls for ten years because you said you knew they would be permitted somewhere up the line."

Put simply, disregard for liturgical law—whether coming from the left or the right—must be dealt with if we are to have a liturgy that is sacred, closed to political influence, and conducive to the peace of the Church.

11. Pseudo-Sophistication

One of the most justified gripes against the liturgical reform is the charge of an inordinately verbal/cerebral approach to worship. We are awash in words and short on symbols—and that is not the Catholic way. The Protestant reformers shied away from signs and symbols because, whether consciously or not, they had a fear of the Incarnation. Catholic sensibilities have always been very keen on celebrating the beauty of created things and their ability to move us beyond to their Creator—and ours. The Baroque in art, architecture, and music was the Catholic response to Protestant skittishness with beauty. Nowadays, we often come up against a mindset that suggests that what cannot be quantified, objectified, and analyzed is little more than magic, superstition, or peasant spirituality. Pascal was right to warn us that "the heart has reasons the mind knows not of." In good catechesis, in good liturgy, as in all fully human experiences of life, there is not, nor should there ever be, any dichotomy between the head and the heart; they are intimately, inextricably related and mutually reinforcing.

12. An Attitude of "I Know Better Than the Church"

This frame of mind is devastating. The sacred liturgy is the possession of the whole Church and not the hobbyhorse of any individual or group. When discussion is going on about proposed changes, every qualified person has the right to participate in the conversation. Once a text or ritual is decided upon by competent authority, the issue is settled and demands compliance. That does not mean that I leave my own critical faculties at the church door, but it does mean that I will refrain from imposing my private judgments on the rest of the Church in the liturgical setting. I certainly have the right—and even the responsibility—to continue to present the rationale for my position in appropriate forums and even to press for a change, but that does not translate into license to "do my own thing" during the Church's worship. Where legitimate options exist, I have the right to opt for my preference, and no liturgical bureaucrats can take away such an option.

The "I know better" syndrome cuts across all ideological lines. It is demonstrated by the priest, cantor, or lector who insists on tinkering with texts so as to make them "inclusive"; it is apparent in the actions of a priest who is determined to reintroduce Tridentine rubrics into the revised rite of the Mass, with the excuse that the General Instruction does not specifically forbid such additions—even though we know that rubrics always and only tell us what *to do*, not what *not to do*. Catholics are not "Lone Rangers"; that is the Protestant principle, writ large. Our paramount concern is the communal good, advancing that for the sake of unity, peace, and the safeguarding of the rights of all.

13. Antiquarianism/Trendiness

Many observers have remarked that so-called liberals and conservatives have much more in common than they would like to admit. One wit said of an arch-conservative priest-friend, "He's gone so far to the right that he's on the left." In liturgical matters, it is not uncommon to hear proponents of a particular practice imagine that they have secured their argument with the line, "And it was done that way in the Early Church." In *Mediator Dei*, the landmark liturgical encyclical of Pope Pius XII, the Church was cautioned against "antiquarianism". We judge something on the basis of its value, not its age. Therefore, simply because something is old does not necessarily mean that it is good. Trendiness makes the opposite presumption, and it is equally wrong.

I must say I am amused by people who push for particular liturgical innovations on the grounds that such things are "ancient". I reply by asking, "If you favor Communion-in-the-hand for that reason, are you also ready to accept public confession of sins, confession once in a lifetime, and life-long penance? That is all ancient, too." No, our principle of discrimination must be far deeper than that. If something existed in the Early Church and was eliminated, we need to ask why it was eliminated; if conditions have changed today, so that the abuse is no longer possible and a great good can accrue to the worship of the faithful, by all means, let us talk about it. If something has never existed before, can we foresee the implications upon its introduction at the levels of theology, spirituality, psychology, and sociology? If all those areas give us green lights, again, let us discuss the matter.

To the shallow partisans of antiquarianism and trendiness alike, I echo Shakespeare: "A plague on both your houses."

Conclusion

Well, we have come to the end of my laundry list; I am sure that I have written things some will agree with; I suspect I have also written some things others may deplore; and undoubtedly I have left out some "pet peeves". But this has been more than a thrashing out of annoying practices or a big wish list. I have thought long and hard about matters liturgical and sacramental over the years, coming at them from a variety of perspectives in theology, sociology, pedagogy, psychology, and pastoral practice. Because truth is one, all the various disciplines should lead us to a stronger hold on it, for everything is interrelated. To the extent that we perceive the "connectedness" of the Catholic vision of truth and life, we shall experience the full meaning of the sacraments. Vagueness, fogginess, and confusion in one area, on the other hand, undermine the overall picture, depriving us of clarity and sharpness of focus.

I think it fair to say that when people outside the Church think about Catholics, invariably their thoughts turn to our constant involvement with the sacraments. And rightly so. Yet the question still imposes itself: Why this preoccupation with sacraments? Sixteen centuries ago, St. Ambrose put it succinctly and powerfully: "You have shown yourself to me face to face, O Christ; it is in your sacraments that I meet you." May that always be so for us as well—and evermore, until time becomes eternity.